Frederick Albion Ober

Mexican Resources

A Guide to And Through Mexico

Frederick Albion Ober

Mexican Resources
A Guide to And Through Mexico

ISBN/EAN: 9783744758963

Printed in Europe, USA, Canada, Australia, Japan

Cover: Foto ©Andreas Hilbeck / pixelio.de

More available books at **www.hansebooks.com**

MEXICAN RESOURCES:

A Guide

TO AND THROUGH MEXICO.

BY

FREDERICK A. OBER

AUTHOR OF "TRAVELS IN MEXICO," "CAMPS IN THE CARIBBEES," "YOUNG FOLKS' HISTORY OF MEXICO," ETC.

Index of Contents.

INDEX OF ADVERTISERS .... Page 36 of GUIDE.
INDEX OF MAPS AND ILLUSTRATIONS .. Page 36 of GUIDE.
CONTENTS OF RESOURCES AND GUIDE .... Page 37.

BOSTON:
ESTES AND LAURIAT.
1884.

PREFATORY.

The material herein contained was originally intended to be appended to the author's "Travels in Mexico," as it in a measure completes and rounds out the larger volume; but the limitations of space and the relentless veto of publishers prevented. There is no repetition. The aim of the work is to present an exact statement of Mexico's natural resources, drawn from reliable statistical works, — such as the *Estadistica de la Republica Mexicana*, — collated, and mainly translated, by the author. The facts are given without exaggeration, at the same time without depreciation; and the reader may draw his own deductions as to Mexico's future from this accurate presentation of her past.

The soil, climate, and productions are shown, of every section, with distinctive features; the great coffee, sugar, and cotton districts, with a full list of all the precious dye and cabinet woods, delicious fruits, and medicinal plants, which make tropical Mexico so valuable a neighbor to the United States.

Under "Mines and Mining" are given the locations of the great deposits of precious metals; abstracts from the mining laws of Mexico, for the guidance of those desiring to locate mines; and full information on the exact localities of the gold, silver, copper, iron, lead, quicksilver, and coal deposits, and the valuable Mexican minerals.

An extensive GUIDE is added, showing every point of importance on every railroad running into and through Mexico, with time and distance tables, and a list of attractions to tourists. There being no longer any Great West to which trade and travel may flow, it is believed that the country of the future lies in the South, — in Mexico, Central and South America.

This book, then, is offered as an indication of what may be found there, and as a guide by the way.

It is not perfect; it is not exhaustive; and it doubtless contains errors which it will be the aim of the author to correct in subsequent editions.

In this first edition, ten thousand copies are issued, at a price nearly nominal, so that it shall have an immediate and wide circulation.

TOURISTS AND TRAVELERS!

BEFORE YOU START,
SECURE AN
ACCIDENT POLICY OR TICKET
IN

THE
TRAVELERS,

OF HARTFORD, CONN.

Only Strong Accident Company in America,
AND BY FAR THE
Largest in the World.

Rates as low as will permanently secure *full payment* of the *face value* of Policies.

Assets, $7,435,000,
Surplus to Policy-holders, $1,868,000.

OUR ACCIDENT POLICIES indemnify the business or professional man for his profits, the wage-worker for his wages lost from accidental injury, and guarantee principal sum in case of death. Our payments to policy-holders last year alone were over *$1,154,000*, of which $864,000 was under Accident Policies.

Only *$5* per year for professional and business men, and office-workers generally, secures *$1,000* in event of death by accident, *$5* per week if disabled. Larger sums at proportionate rates.

Over *one in ten of all Insured* have been killed or injured by accident, and received *cash benefits* from us amounting to over *$6,750,000*.

REGISTERED ACCIDENT TICKETS,
Just the thing for Travelers, but not limited to Accidents of Travel,
Sold at Local Agencies and Railroad Stations.

25 cents a day, *$4.50* for thirty days, secures *$3,000* in case of death, *$15* a week if disabled.

J. G. BATTERSON, President.   RODNEY DENNIS, Secretary.
JOHN E. MORRIS, Assistant Secretary.

MEXICAN RESOURCES.

AREA.

THE territory of the Mexican Republic extends from north latitude 15° to 32°; and from 12° 18′ 46″ of east longitude, to 18° 6′ 15″ of west longitude of the meridian of the City of Mexico, the capital; this being in west longitude from Greenwich, 99° 5′ 25″. The territory contiguous on the north belongs to the United States, and that on the south to Guatemala, while the Gulf of Mexico bathes its eastern shores, and the Pacific its western, giving to it a coast-line of nearly 6,000 miles. Within the above limits is inclosed a superficial area of 1,958,912 square kilometres, or 766,000 square miles. Its greatest length, along the axis of the territory, mainly represented by the gigantic dorsal ridge of the Sierra Madre, is 1,970 miles, in a straight line from the northwestern extremity of Lower California to the southern border of Chiapas. Its maximum breadth, from east to west, on the line of north latitude 26°, is about 750 miles, and its minimum, at the Isthmus of Tehuantepec, 140 miles.

BOUNDARIES.

In ancient times New Spain included the territory lying between north latitude 15° and 42°. By the treaty between Spain and the United States (Feb. 22, 1819), the boundary was defined as commencing at the mouth of the Sabine River of Texas. By the Treaty of Guadalupe (Feb. 2, 1848), the Rio Grande, or Rio Bravo del Norte, forms the division between Mexico and the United States, starting at a point three leagues from its mouth. By the "Gadsden Purchase" Convention, 1853, the United States received a further addition of Mexican territory, amounting to 45,535 square miles. The dividing line between the two republics now follows the course of the Rio Grande, north, to north latitude 31° 47′, thence 100 miles westward on the same parallel, whence it runs south to parallel 31° 11′, follows this line to meridian 111° from Greenwich, thence northwest to the Rio Colorado, and up that river to the boundary between Upper and Lower California, which is followed to a point south of San Diego, on the Pacific. Prior to the treaty of 1848, it was estimated that the area of Mexico was over 1,650,000 square miles; but, by comparison, it will be seen that the United States gained over half this territory, by an excess of 100,000 square miles.

CONFIGURATION OF THE COAST.

Although the plains of the coast-region are low, the greatest portion of Mexico lies high above the sea. Of its 6,000 miles of coast-line, about 1,600 pertain to the Atlantic or Gulf of Mexico; and 4,200 to the Pacific and Gulf of California. Very few bays indent the coast. These are, Ascension, Espiritu Santo, and Chetmul on the Yucutan Peninsula; Manzanillo, on the Pacific; and Magdalena and others in Lower California. But the east coast is broken by extensive lagoons, like that of Terminos, and the great Gulf of California separates the peninsula of that name from the main portion of Mexico. Of secure harbors, there are none on the east coast, and but very few on the west,—Acapulco, San Blas and Guaymas, being the only inlets with deep water and protecting shores. The ports of Mexico, open to foreign commerce, are: on the Pacific, Acapulco, Guaymas, La Paz (Lower California), Mazatlan, Manzanillo, Puerto Angel, Salina Cruz, San Blas, Soconusco and Tonalá. Open to coastwise trade, only: Altata, Bacorchuis, Cabo de San Lucas, Mulegé, Navachiste, Navidad, Puerto Escondido, Tecoanapa, Topolovampo, Valle de Banderas, Yavaros and Zihuatanejo. On the Gulf of Mexico, open to foreign commerce, are: Anton Lizardo, Campeche, Carmen, Goatzacoalcos, Frontera, Progreso, Tampico, Tuxpan and Vera Cruz. To the coasting-trade: Alvarado, Dos Bocas, Nautla, Soto la Marina, Santecomapan and Tecolutla.

The only peninsulas are Lower California and Yucatan; which latter belongs to Mexico politically, but physically is widely separate from it. Several islands, though of little importance, lie off its coasts.

PHYSICAL FEATURES OF THE PLATEAUX.

Generally speaking, the main body of the Mexican territory is a vast table-land, a distinct geographical region, traversed by mountain-chains of great length, and rising to extraordinary heights. Leaving out Yucatan and contiguous country, we may describe Mexico as consisting of a series of plateaux, lying mainly above a height of 6,000 feet; extending from the confines of Guatemala, to the northern limit of its boundary-line; falling abruptly towards the coast on either hand, and descending gradually to the plains of Texas and Arizona in the north.

In the south, we have the Valley of Oaxaca, 4,500 feet; next of Pueblo, about 7,000 feet; of Anahuac, 7,500 feet; and, going north, along the axis of this tableland, find Durango at an altitude of 6,600 feet; Chihuahua, 4,600 feet; El Paso, 3,800 feet, while Santa Fé, New Mexico, again lies at 7,000 feet above the sea. The extent of the plateaux is about 1,500 miles in length, by 500 miles in breadth. Of the vast mountain system, forming the escarpment to this elevated region, the Sierra Madre, of the Pacific coast, the great "Mother Range," is the longest continuous chain, extending from the Isthmus of Tehuantepec to Arizona. The eastern Cordillera, or chain, runs more directly northward, from its initial point, and at a lesser mean elevation, of, perhaps, 6,000 feet; while the western carries an altitude of nearly 10,000 feet.

Traversing this longitudinal system from east to west, are several cross-ridges, due to igneous action, and containing some of the highest volcanoes in North America. Of the numerous mountains that rise conspicuously above the plateaux, there are twenty above 4,000 feet in height, and nine that surpass even 10,000 feet.

These are, as given by the Mexican geographer, Cubas: Popocatapetl, 5,400 metres; Orizaba, 5,295; Iztaccihuatl, 4,775; Nevada de Toluca, 4,440; Cofre de Perote, 4,089; Zempoaltepetl, 3,668; Ajusco, 3,575; Volcan de Colima, 3,396, and Quinceo, 3,324 metres. "The most interesting feature of the distribution of volcanoes," says a learned writer, "is that nearly all are situated along the mountain-chains and rows of islands which border the shores of the continent, while the interior of these great land masses is nearly free from them." This seems to be exceptional in Mexico, as the highest and most noted volcanoes, as Popocatapetl, Nevada de Toluca, Cofre de Perote and Jorullo, are in the centre of the table-land, and traverse the country in a line from west to east. All the Mexican volcanoes are either extinct or quiescent; none have been in eruption in the present century, though smoke has been seen issuing from the crater of Popocatapetl.

The Mexican river system, owing to the rugged configuration of the surface, is neither varied nor extensive. Most of the rivers are short, and little more than impetuous torrents or sluggish bayous, without navigable depth of water. The steep mountain-slopes are quickly drained, and the great plateaux rapidly absorb the waters that fall into them, owing to their aridity. The surface of the table-land is cut up into innumerable barrancas and ravines, some of profound depth, caused by the plunging torrents, speeding on their way to the sea. Since the comprehensive railway system of Mexico has been projected, the canalization of Mexico will not be needed, nor will the almost total lack of navigable waters be sorely felt. Even the longest streams (such as the Rio Grande, which forms the boundary line between Mexico and Texas, and is about 1,500 miles in length), are navigable for but a short distance. There are some twenty rivers above one hundred miles long, the principal of which are: the Rio Grande, the Santiago, 500 miles; the Balsas, 400; Yaquis, 375; Grijalva, or Tabasco, 330; Usumacinta, 320; Conchos, 300; Mezqintal, 310; Panuco, 275; Altar, 260; Nazas, 260; Sinaloa, 250; Fuerte, 240; Mayo, 200; Ures, 200; Alvarado, 150; Culiacan, 150; and Goatzcoalcos, 140 miles.

The number of lakes in Mexico is very small, and may be counted upon one's fingers. Leaving out the lagunas, which are merely bodies of salt water separated from the Gulf by sand-banks and shoals, we find not more than ten inland lakes. These are, the five lakes and ponds of the Valley of Mexico: Tezcoco, Chalco, Xochimilco, Xaltocan, and Zumpanzo; Chapala, the largest in Mexico, having an estimated area of 1,300 square miles, situated in Jalisco; two or three small bodies in the laguna country, in Chihuahua and southwest Coahuila. The lacustrine basins, though of sufficient area, are so arid and so exposed to the influences of a hot climate, at a great altitude, that evaporation is rapid, and causes the total disappearance of many streams and even lakes.

CLIMATE AND SEASONS.

So intimately connected are climate and vegetation, that to indicate the variations of the one is to suggest a corresponding change in the flora of the country.

Were Mexico nearly level from gulf to ocean, it would have mainly a tropical climate, as it lies to a great extent south of the northern tropic; but, owing to physical causes, a large area of its territory enjoys the climate of the temperate zone. Rising by successive stages to a height of nearly 18,000 feet, the temperature, of course, undergoes a diminution corresponding with the elevation above the sea.

Thus the coast, for quite its entire length, is hot, and much of it extremely unhealthy. The low-lying region appertaining to it is well designated the *tierra caliente*, or "hot country," in which the humid atmosphere perpetually nourishes a vegetation peculiarly tropical. The mean annual temperature of this climatic zone ranges from 75° to 82° (Fahr.), the extremes being from about 55° to 105°. Its influence is felt to an approximate altitude of about 3,000 feet above the sea. It may be safely visited, as a rule, between the months of December and April, when the heated coast is subject to violent gales called northers — *los nortes*, which cool the air, and dissipate the germs of disease. At an altitude above sea-level of about 3,000 feet, we enter the *tierra templada*, the "temperate country," where the average mean annual temperature is about 70°, and the extremes 50° to 86°. Extremes in temperature are almost unknown in this zone, a delightful coolness prevailing in the shade, while the vegetable forms, though not entirely characteristic, blending as they do those of both the lower and upper regions, are of most astonishing variety.

The prevailing climate of the *tierra templada* is warm and moist, the precipitation from the clouds from the Gulf (on the eastern coast) being great, and the rainfall greater than either in the higher, or the lower zone. The classification is an arbitrary one, and it is difficult to say just at what elevation each zone overlaps and merges into the other; but it may be roughly stated that the *tierra caliente* extends upward from the coast to a vertical height of 3,000 feet, the *templada* from 3,000 to 7,000 or 8,000, — the verge of the table-land, — while above that altitude is the *tierra fria*, or "cold region," with a vegetation varying from the corn and barley, and maguey of the lower levels to the cryptogamia of the mountain-tops. The mean annual temperature of the *tierra fria*, which includes the greater portion of the vast plateau, is about 60°, the extremes reaching from 75° to the freezing-point. Travel on the table-land may be equally agreeable, summer or winter, excepting that it is liable to frequent detentions during the rainy season.

The Mexicans divide the year into two periods: *el estio*, or the dry season, and *la estacion de las aguas*, or the rainy season. The latter comprises the months of June, July, August, and September, while the dry season extends over the greater portion of the rest of the year. "The curving shores of Mexico along the Gulf and interior highlands gather and hem in an immense body of vapor, which is carried on by the trade-winds, and condensed against the cold and lofty inland mountain-peaks which rise above the limit of perpetual congelation. This occurs during the dry season, whilst the sun is at the south. But when its power increases, as it advances northward, and until it has long turned back again on its southern course, these vapors are dissolved by the hot intertropical air, and descend almost daily in fertilizing showers."

Electric storms and water-spouts rarely occur, except in certain well-determined localities, as at various points on the coast. Earthquakes are infrequent, and seldom destructive, being rather *temblores*, or tremblings, than *terremotos*, or shakings.

The duration of the day, in winter, including morning and evening twilight, is 12 hours 35' to 13 hours 40'; in spring, 14 hours 36' to 15 hours 38'; in summer, 15 hours 54' to 16 hours 44'; and in autumn, 13 hours 52' to 14 hours 46'.

ZONES OF VEGETATION.

Although the indigenous plants of Mexico are by no means few in number, it now possesses, undoubtedly, through its Old World acquisitions, the richest economic flora of any country on the globe. This is owing to the fact that a goodly portion of Mexico lies within the tropics, and at the same time attains to a great elevation above the sea; in other words, *altitude* confers upon this elevated region beneath the northern tropic all the variety of climate that one would meet with in journeying from the equator to the pole. The vegetable world, says the German writer Sartorius, is of course always determined by the nature of the soil; on a calcareous soil we find a different description of plants to those which are met with in trachyte or porphyry; for instance, in lime we have chiefly fan palms and malvaceæ: but the conditions which the elevation above the sea produce, the *isothermal line*, would everywhere call forth analogous appearances.

The Old World has sent here its apples, pears, cherries, peaches, oranges, figs, grapes, and pomegranates; by their side flourish the East Indian mangoes, papaws, the American ananas (6 species), mammees, aguacates, spondias, the fruit of the passion-flower, excellent cactus fruits, gourds of all kinds, and many others.

"An Indian village of the temperate zone, where coast and hill country meet and blend, presents a truly delightful picture, surrounded by heavily-laden orange-trees and banana-stalks, by fruits of every imaginable hue, and by the blossoming shrubs which invariably follow the steps of man."

In the lower, or coast, regions, as high as 1,500 feet, we have coconuts, cacao, vanilla, cotton, cloves, nutmegs, peppers, and the other spices of commerce, besides all the fruits of the tropical countries of the East and West. Up to 4,000 feet grow sugar and coffee, indigo, rice, tea, banana, and tobacco, besides the productive edible roots: manioc, yam, arum, arrow-root, sweet potato, curcuma and ginger, and all the fruits of America, Central Asia, and Barbary. From this point upwards begins the cultivation of the cerealia of the Old World, such as barley and wheat, of the oleaginous plants (olive, poppy, rape, and linseed) of pulse and kitchen vegetables, of grapes for wine, and every kind of European fruit. The mulberry tree finds its climate at the height of from 3,000 to 6,000 feet above the sea.

From the following partial catalogue of the fruits and vegetables cultivated in Mexico, one may be led to believe in its agricultural possibilities. It was Humboldt who estimated the value of the gold and silver of the Mexican mines at the beginning of this century, vast as it was, as less by almost a fourth than that of the territorial produce. Mexico, as its national statistician very truly remarks, has the markets of all the world constantly open for the excess of her agricultural productions, for, such is the varied nature of her soil and climate, that there is scarcely a plant that grows, or a fruit that ripens, or a grain that matures its seed, that may not find a congenial home within her limits. Plants of the different zones, from frigid to torrid, are all found in the ascent from coast to table-land, and indicate to a nicety the different degrees of altitude and temperature.

Not only can she export many of the cereals, but she has almost a monopoly of several peculiar products of the tropics, and, owing to the combined advantages of topography and climate, can supply foreign markets with immense quantities of such valuable articles as coffee, cacao, henequen, tobacco, vanilla, and precious woods.

MEXICO'S ECONOMIC FLORA

Under this distinctive title, while no attempt has been made to compile an exhaustive botanical catalogue, — which would be quite unnecessary, even if practicable,—the author here presents statistics valuable to those interested in the *industrial possibilities* of Mexico. This information has been obtained almost entirely from Mexican sources, and, though perhaps incomplete, is at least an approach to that accuracy so desirable in a statement of Mexico's material resources, and valuable as an offset to the misrepresentations of misinformed or prejudiced writers.

Many of the names in the following list, being native to the country, generally Aztec, are not found in any Spanish dictionary; but all the most important woods, fruits, etc., are given, with not only the indigenous appellations, but their English equivalents. The flora of Mexico is rich and varied, embracing, says its statistician, over ten thousand species, known and analyzed. Her woods are valuable, a great number of her native plants have medicinal qualities, and her flowers are beautiful and of exquisite fragrance.

These lists comprise mainly those Mexican plants valuable for their properties, and those interesting from flowering at a great altitude, and typical of the tablelands; a strictly scientific classification has not been adopted, as this would have been impracticable.

TIMBER AND CONSTRUCTION WOODS.

Mexican Name.	English.	Mexican Name.	English.
Ahuehuete.	Cypress.	Majahua.	(Bark is used for cordage).
Aile.			
Alamo.	Poplar (3 species).	Mangle.	Mangrove.
Acana.	A hard, reddish wood.	Mango.	Mango.
Amate.		Nogal.	Walnut (2 species).
Capire.	Black and yellow.	Olmo.	Elm.
Capulin.	Tree with fruit resembling cherry.	Ocuna.	
		Palo Dulce, de Maria, morado mora, bravo, colorado y de hierro.	Licorice, violet, mulberry, redwood, ironwood, etc.
Capulincillo.	Do. do.		
Cedro.	Cedar (3 species).		
Ciprés.	Cypress.	Pareta.	
Ceiba ó pochote.	Silk cotton.	Pino.	White, resinous, and red pine.
Castaño.	Chestnut.		
Canté.		Pinavete.	
Ciruelo.	Plum.	Perú.	
Encino.	Oak (white, black, and yellow).	Quiebra hacha.	Break-axe.
		Roble (blanco y encino.	Oak (white and evergreen).
Fresno.	Ash.		
Fresnillo.	Little Ash.	Sabino.	Sabin.
Frijolillo.		Sauz, verde, blanco, y mexicano.	Willow (green, white, Mexican).
Guachipilino.			
Guamuchil.		Suchil.	
Guásima.		Sabicú.	
Garrapata.	Tick-tree.	Tamarindo.	Tamarind.
Garrapatilla.	Little tick-tree.	Taray.	Tamarisk.
Haya.	Beech.	Tampincerán.	
Huitzache.		Tepehuaje.	
Hoba.		Tlaliscuahuitl.	
Hasta.		Tepozan.	
Jahua.		Tecomate.	Gourd-tree.
Mamey.	Mammee-tree.	Zaya.	
Madroño.	Strawberry-tree.	Zopilote.	

THE TROPICAL FORESTS.

We find in profusion, in the tropical forests of southern Mexico, those valuable woods which are only seen beneath the almost vertical sun of the Tropics. It will be seen that Mexico has not less than twenty varieties of wood, useful in the joiner-work, and for interior furnishing, while about sixty are enumerated as in use for timber. In effect, Mexico has all the useful timber-trees of the North, with all the added precious woods of the South. Among woods noted for their fineness of grain, and susceptibility to polish, may be mentioned: ebony, lignum-vitæ, mahogany, manchinille, rosewood, sapota and violet-wood. Among trees famous for their size, and the durability of their wood, are the cedars, cypresses, ceibas, or silk-cottons, chestnuts, oaks, pines, tamarinds, tamarisks, etc., etc., — a long list.

CABINET AND DYE WOODS.

Mexican Name.	English.	Mexican Name.	English.
Avellano.	Hazel.	Primavera.	Primrose.
Almendro.	Almond.	Zapote blanco.	Sapota (white).
Bálsamo.	Balsam.	Zapote prieto.	Sapota (blackish).
Boa.		Añil.	Indigo.
Caoba.	Mahogany.	Agrita.	
Caobilla.	Little Mahogany	Achiote.	Arnatto.
Ébano.	Ebony.	Brasil.	Brazil-wood.
Granadillo.	Passion flower.	Campeche.	Logwood.
Guachichil.	(A hard wood.)	Cascalote.	
Guamuchil.		Ébano verde.	Green ebony.
Ilamo.		Huitzache (fruit).	
Linaloé.	Aloes-tree.	Lentisco.	Mastic.
Laurel.	Laurel.	Mangle.	Mangrove.
Lloron (Sauce).	Weeping willow.	Palo amarillo.	Fustic.
Manzanilla.	Manchinille.	Palo mulato.	Tawney wood.
Ojo de Pájaro.	Bird's-eye.	Timbra.	Mountain hyssop.
Palo morado.	Violet wood.	Azafran.	Saffron.
Palo de rosa.	Rosewood.	Orchilla.	Archil.
Palo santo.	Lignum vitæ.	Rubia (*raiz de tinta*).	Madder.

GUM, RESIN, AND OIL-YIELDING PLANTS.

Mexican Name.	English.	Mexican Name.	English.
Almácigo.	Mastic.	Alegria.	Oily grain.
Drago.	Dragon-tree.	Almendro (fruit).	Almond.
Mezquite.	(Its gum is equal to gum-arabic.)	Cacahuate.	Pea-nut.
		Chia.	Lime-leaved sage.
Hule.	Caoutchouc.	Coacoyutl (fruit).	
Ambar amarillo.	Amber (yellow).	Coco (fruit).	Coco palm.
Copal.	Copal.	Nogal (fruit).	Walnut.
Copalchi.	Liquid amber.	Nuez moscada.	Nutmeg.
Pino de trementina.	Turpentine-tree.	Olivo (fruit).	Olive.
Abeto.	Silver-tree.	Linaza.	Linseed.
Acebuche.	Wild olive.	Nabo.	Rape.
Ajonjoli.	Beneseed.		

CEREALS, ALIMENTAL PLANTS, ETC.

Mexican Name.	English.	Mexican Name.	English.
Apio.	Celery.	Chile.	Red pepper (many kinds).
Alcancil or Alcachofa.	Artichoke.	Escarola (lechuga china).	Endive.
Acedera.	Sorrel.	Espárrago.	Asparagus.
Aceituna.	Olives.	Espinaca.	Spinage.
Acelga.	Beet.	Frijole.	Beans; French beans.
Alcaparra.	Caper.	Garbanzo.	Chick pea.
Ajo.	Garlic.	Haba.	Garden beans.
Alverjon.	Vetch.	Hejotes.	String beans.
Arroz.	Rice.	Lechuga.	Lettuce.
Brocoli.	Broccoli.	Lenteja.	Lentil.
Berengena.	Egg-plant.	Maguey.	American agave.
Brichuela.		Maiz.	Corn (every variety).
Cacao.	Cocoa.	Nabo.	Rape.
Café.	Coffee.	Name.	
Comino.	Cumin Seed.	Papa.	Potato.
Col ó repollo.	Cabbage.	Pepino.	Cucumber.
Coliflor.	Cauliflower.	Puerro.	Leek.
Calabazas.	Pumpkins, gourds, etc.	Perejil.	Parsley.
Caña de azúcar.	Sugar-cane.	Pimienta.	Pepper.
Cardo.	Garden artichoke.	Rábano.	Radish.
Camote.	Sweet potato.	Trigo.	Wheat.
Cebada.	Barley.	Verdolaga	Purslain.
Cebolla.	Onion.	Yuca ó guacamote.	Yucca.
Chayote.		Zanahoria.	Carrot.

TEXTILES.

Mexican Name.	English.	Mexican Name.	English.
Algodon.	Cotton.	Lino.	Flax.
Cañamo.	Hemp.	Ramié — Ramee.	China grass.
Henequen.	Sisal hemp.	Seda vegetal	Vegetable silk.
Ixtle.	Aloe fibre.		

It will only be necessary to call attention to the following list, to have it made evident that there is hardly a fruit in the known world that has not found, or cannot find, a congenial home in Mexico.

The most valuable, and those least known to dwellers in the north, will be found described after their respective appellations. To mention all would be to enumerate nearly every variety cultivated in both habitable zones, and far exceed the limits of this work, or, indeed, of any book not specially devoted to horticulture.

While every fruit can be grown in Mexico, it is a well-known fact that those indigenous to other countries do not here preserve their original fine flavor, the peaches, pears, etc., being hard, coarse, and, in a measure, flavorless.

THE FRUITS OF MEXICO.

Mexican Name.	English.	Mexican Name.	English.
Ahuacate.	A delicious American fruit.	Madroño.	Strawberry-tree.
		Melon comun.	Melon.
Albérchigo.	Peach.	Melon de agua.	Water-melon.
Albericoque.	Apricot.	Melon de olor.	Musk-melon.
Anona.	Custard apple.	Melon zapote.	Sapote-melon.
Arrayan.	Myrtle.	Mamey.	Mammee.
Breva.	Variety of fig.	Nanche.	
Caimito blanco.		Naranja de China.	Orange (China).
Caimito morado.		Naranja ágria.	Orange (sour).
Capulin, blanco y negro.	American cherry.	Nuez de Castilla.	Spanish walnut.
Cereza.	Cherry.	Níspero.	Medlar-tree.
Coco.	Coco-nut.	Prisco.	A kind of peach.
Castaña.	Chestnut.	Piña.	Pine-nut.
Cidra.	Citron.	Poma rosa.	Rose-apple.
Ciruela.	Plums (all varieties).	Peras (de nueve clases).	Pears (nine varieties).
Cuaginicuil.		Pingüica.	Oil-nut.
Chabacano.	A kind of apricot.	Papaya.	Papaw.
Chirimoya.		Pitahaya.	Giant cactus.
Chicozapote.		Pachona.	
Damasco.	Damson.	Plátano grande.	Plantain tree.
Durazno.	Peach.	Plátano guineo.	Plantain (Guinea).
Dátil.	Date.	Plátano manilo.	Plantain (Manilla).
Fresa.	Strawberry.	Plátano manzano.	Plantain (Apple).
Grosella.	Currant.	Sandia.	A Water-melon.
Garambullo.		Tejocote.	
Guanavana.		Tuna blanca.	Tuna (White), Indian fig, or prickly-pear.
Granada China.	Pomegranate.		
Guinda.	A cherry.	Tuna amarilla.	Tuna (yellow).
Guayaba.	Guava.	Tuna encarnada.	Tuna (pink).
Higo.	Indian fig.	Tuna cardona.	Cochineal cactus.
Hilama.	A chirimoya.	Uva.	Grape (all varieties).
Hicaco.		Uva blanca.	Grape (white).
Jícama.	Farinaceous root.	Uva moscatel.	Grape (fox).
Lima.	Lime.	Uva negra.	Grape (black).
Limon ágrio.	Lemon (sour).	Uva silvestre.	Grape (wild).
Limon dulce.	Lemon (sweet).	Zarzamora.	Blackberry.
Limoncillo.	Little lemon.	Zapote blanco.	Sapota (white).
Mango.	Mango.	Zapote negro.	Sapota (black).
Manzanas.	Apples (seven varieties).	Zapote amarillo.	Sapota (yellow).
Membrillo.	Quince.	Zapotillo.	Little sapota.
Mora.	Mulberry.		

MEDICINAL PLANTS.

Mexican Name.	English.	Mexican Name.	English.
Adornidera.	Poppy.	Marihuana.	
Anacahuite.		Manzanilla.	Chamomile.
Amapola.	Poppy.	Mejorana.	Sweet marjoram.
Ajenjo.	Wormwood.	Mostaza.	Mustard.
Apio.	Celery.	Morera.	Mulberry.
Artemesa.	Mug-wort.	Maravilla.	Heliotrope.
Albahaca.	Sweet basil.	Mezquite.	
Alhuçema.	Lavender.	Mixtamazuchil.	
Altea.	Marshmallow.	Neldo.	
Achicoria.		Orozuz.	Licorice.
Alfilerillo.		Ojo de perico.	Parrot's eye.
Arrayan.	Myrtle.	Palo mulato del salvaje.	
Anis.	Anise.	Poléo.	Pennyroyal.
Azafran del pais.	Saffron (native).	Perejil.	Parsley.
Ajenjabe.	Wild mustard.	Peonia.	Peony.
Betonica.	Betony.	Pimienta.	Pepper.
Borraja.	Borage.	Papaloquelite.	
Beleño.	Henbane.	Pata de Leon.	Lion's foot.
Berro.	Water-cress.	Pastora.	
Culantrillo.	Maiden's hair.	Paretaria.	
Canchalahua.		Pipitzahua.	
Cicuta.	Hemlock.	Ruda.	Rue.
Centaura.	Centaury.	Rosa de Páscua.	Easter-rose.
Capitaneja.		Rosa laurel.	
Cohombro.	Snake cucumber.	Quina.	Cinchona.
Calahuala.	Calaguala.	Romero.	Rosemary.
Cañafistula.	Cassia fistula.	Sasafras.	Sassafras.
Canuela.	Fescue grass.	Siempreviva.	House-leek (red and yellow).
Cuchalate.			
Calabaza chicayota.	Calabash.	Sabina.	Savin.
Contrayerba.		Salvia.	Sage.
Cardo santo.	Holy thistle.	Sauco blanco.	Elder.
Cebadilla.	Cevadilla.	Sanguinaria.	Knot-grass.
Damiana.		Tamarindo.	Tamarind.
Digital.	Foxglove.	Tianguispepetla.	
Escorzonera.	Viper-root.	Trompetilla.	
Espinosilla.		Torongil.	Balm.
Fresno.	Ash.	Tornillo.	
Genciana.	Gentian.	Trebol.	Trefoil.
Gordolobo.	Mullein.	Tlacopatle.	
Guayacan.	Lignum vitæ.	Té silvestre.	Wild tea.
Hinojo.	Fennel.	Tilia.	Lime-tree.
Higuerilla.	Castor-oil plant.	Tabaco.	Tobacco.
Incienso.	Incense (gum).	Vainilla.	Vanilla.
Ipecacuana.	Ipecacuanha.	Valeriana.	Valerian.
Jalapa.	Jalap.	Verbena.	Vervain.
Lupulo.	Hops.	Verdolaga.	Purslane.
Laurel.	Laurel.	Yerba buena.	Mint.
Linaza.	Flaxseed.	Yerba del pollo.	
Limoncillo.	Lime.	Yerba del zapo.	
Lengua de cierro.	Hart's tongue.	Yerba de la golondrina.	
Manrubio.		Yoloxuchil.	
Mastuerzo.	Cress.	Zarzaparilla.	Sarsaparilla.
Malva.	Mallow.	Zumpanitl.	

FLOWERS AND ORNAMENTAL PLANTS.

Following is a partial list of the flowers, mainly European, cultivated in the Mexican gardens.

Mexican Name.	English.	Mexican Name.	English.
Acacia comun.	Acacia.	Dulcamara.	Bitter-sweet.
Acanto.	Thistle.	Encina olorosa.	Oily evergreen oak.
Adelfa.	Rose-bay.	Espino blanco.	Whitethorn.
Ajenjo.	Wormwood.	Espino rosado.	Buckthorn.
Alelí.	Gilliflower.	Floripundo.	Magnolia.
Ambrosía.	Buckthorn.	Geranio olorosa.	Cranesbill.
Anana.	Pineapple.	Helecho.	Fern-filex.
Alhucema.	Lavender.	Heliótropo.	Heliotrope.
Anémona.	Anemones.	Heptáica.	Liverwort.
Ápio.	Celery.	Immortal.	Inmortal.
Argentina.	Satin cinquefoil.	Jacinto.	Hyacinth (four species).
Artemisa.	Artemisia.	Lirio blanco.	Florentine iris.
Azahar de naranjo.	Orange flower.	Lila blanca.	Lilac (white).
Azahar de limon.	Lemon flower.	Madre-selva.	Honeysuckle.
Azahar de lima.	Lime flower.	Margarita.	
Azahar de cidra.	Citron flower.	Magnolia.	Magnolia.
Azahar de toronja.	Shaddoc flower.	Mirto.	Myrtle.
Azahar de Chirimoya	Anona flower.	Narciso.	Daffodil.
Balsamina.	Balsam-apple.	Nardo.	Tuberose.
Betónica.	Betony.	Peonia.	Peony.
Cacaloxochitl.		Reseda.	
Centaura.	Centaury.	Rosas.	Roses (every variety).
Caléndula.	Marigold.	Sardónia.	Crow-foot.
Camelia.	Camelia.	Serpentaria.	Snake-root.
Campanilla.	Bell-flower.	Tomillo.	Thyme.
Capuchina.	Nasturtium.	Toronjil.	Balm.
Clavel rojo.	Pink (red).	Trinitaria.	Pansy.
Clavel blanco.	Pink (white).	Tuberosa.	Tuberose.
Clavellina.	Mignonette.	Tulipan.	Tulip.
Chícharo or Guisante.	Sweet-pea.	Valeriana.	Valerian.
Dálias.	Dahlias.	Violetas.	Violets (all species).

Among them any flowers which embellish the meads and adorn the gardens of Mexico, says the old historian Clavigero, there are some worthy to be mentioned, either from their singular beauty, or their extraordinary forms. The *Floripundo* merits the first mention, on account of its size, a beautiful white and odoriferous flower, more than eight inches in length and four in diameter. The *Yollocxochitl*, or flower-of-the-heart, is so fragrant that a single one will fill a whole house with its perfume, while the *Coatzontecoxochitl*, or viper's-head, is of incomparable beauty, and highly esteemed by the Mexicans. The *Oceloxochitl*, or tiger-flower, is so called, because spotted like an ocelot, or tiger; the *Cacaloxochitl*, or raven-flower, (the frangipanni), is very odorous, and is made by the Spaniards into conserves; the *Chempoalxochitl*, is the Indian carnation; the *Xiloxochitl*, a beautiful red flower, and the *Macphalxochitl*, or flower-of-the-hand, a most wonderful production of nature, in the form of a bird's foot, or the hand of an ape. Not a flower blossoms in Mexico that has not an expressive Aztec name, so well versed were the aborigines of that country in the lore of the field and forest.

"Besides these, and innumerable other flowers," adds the historian, "which the ancient Mexicans delighted to cultivate, the land has been enriched with all those which could be transported from Asia and Europe, until the gardens of Mexico rival those of the Old World."

The pastures are abundant and nutritious, and in several states, as in Sonora, Tamaulipas and Lower California, are fragrant with aromatic herbs, like the sweet marjoram and wild thyme.

Fournier, the eminent botanist, finds in Mexico six hundred and thirty-eight varieties of grasses, three hundred and seventy-six of which, it is said, occur in no other land. Of the rest, eighty-two are found in the United States.

AZTEC AGRICULTURE,

At the time Mexico was invaded by the Spaniards, was in an advanced state, even if we compare it with European progress at the opening of the fifteenth century.

When, according to tradition, the Toltecs were banished from their native country, — or that in which they had sojourned for a long period, — and began their journey southward, they tarried at certain places, and there erected houses and planted cotton and corn; and in this manner leisurely approached Tula, where they remained many years, and eventually reached the valley of Mexico. The Aztecs, upon their arrival, or at a period subsequent, incorporated into their nation the remains of the scattered Toltec tribes, and gained thereby many arts and processes hitherto unknown to them. It was probably after the founding of the Aztec capital, Tenochtitlan, in 1325, that they made use of the *chinampas*, or floating gardens, upon which they planted vegetables necessary for their subsistence.

In preparing their land for cultivation, they first cut down the trees, and then burned it over, the ashes being, so far as is known, their only fertilizer. They enclosed their fields with walls and hedges of agave, and labored industriously to keep them in good condition. Their implements were few, and of the rudest description, being but a wooden shovel or spade, the *coatl*, or hoe, of copper, with a handle of wood, and a rude knife or sickle of the same metal. In planting, they made a hole with a sharpened stick, into which the seed was dropped, and covered with the foot. They carefully protected their fields from birds and predatory animals, by means of watchmen, and, especially in the *tierra caliente*, — practised irrigation in a most economical and scientific manner. They built granaries and stored vast quantities of corn — their only cereal; besides which, they had beans, *chile*, magueys, pumpkins and gourds, and later, cacao, vanilla, and many other native fruits. While providing themselves with the necessaries of life, they did not neglect the cultivation of those plants usually regarded by the savage as useless: their gardens of flowers and odoriferous plants were the wonder of the Spaniards when they first entered the valley. The markets of Mexico, as the Aztecs became firmly fixed in their valley fortress, and as they extended their conquests to the coasts on either side, became filled with the vegetable production of every zone and climate; as attested by the letters of Cortés, Bernal Diaz, and others.

The Mexicans then had long since passed the dividing line between the rude nomads of the plains and forest, and the patient cultivator of the soil; they were even more than mere herdsmen, had passed beyond the pastoral period, and were firmly fixed in possession of estates. Without beasts of burden, they were obliged to train the lower classes to carry heavy loads, and labor in the field was performed solely by human hands. But they, — even in their necessitous condition, — were more advanced than many nations of Europe, and even than the English, if we may believe one of the earliest of our books on agriculture.

The range of food-plants on the table-land of Mexico was not broad, but the people utilized them all. Maize was their chief reliance, growing everywhere from coast to mountain-top; and from it they prepared a variety of foods and drinks perfectly astonishing. They clothed themselves with cotton, from the tropic coast-belt, drank beverages prepared from the cacao (*chocolatl*), the maguey and the maize, and drew upon the sylvan fauna and flora for a multitude of simple articles of sustenance. While they had no fowls, except the wild turkeys and curassows (*crax alector*), they obtained eggs from iguanas, turtles, alligators, and some native birds; and meat from quail, rabbits, deer, *alcos*, or native dogs, peccaries, and other animals indigenous to the country. Agriculture proper, however, in its most restricted sense, — the tillage of the soil, — furnished them with their principal aliment. Aside from tradition, and the records of the picture-writings, — which some may question, and we will not call in testimony, — "ineffaceable evidence of a high state of agriculture exists all over Mexico." One may still find, on the savannas of the coast, as they extend up towards the hills and mountains, "traces of a dense agricultural population; of tribes who had passed away long before the Spanish invasion; for, when these plains are laid bare by fire, it will be seen that the entire region was formed into terraces, by means of walls of masonry, with every precaution against the ravages of the tropical rains. . . . All is now concealed by trees, or tall grass; for miles, scarcely a hut is built, where formerly every foot of land was as diligently cultivated as the banks of the Nile, or the Euphrates, in Solomon's time."

"In the other Hemisphere," says the historian Herrera, in the quaint English version of his time, "there were no dogs, asses, sheep, goats, swine, cats, horses, mules, camels, nor elephants; no oranges, lemons, pomegranates, figs, quince, olives, melons, vines, sugar, wheat, nor rice."

By indicating what the aboriginal inhabitants of America lacked, we may be better able to show what was accomplished after the Europeans had gained possession of the country. Every variety of soil and climate having been bestowed upon it, a natural dwelling-place could always be found for whatever fruit or vegetable was introduced from the Old World.

Hernando Cortés wrote to his sovereign, shortly after the siege of Mexico: "All the plants of Spain thrive admirably in this land. We shall not proceed here as we have done in the isles (West Indies), where we have neglected cultivation, and destroyed the inhabitants." Unfortunately, both for Spain and for Mexico, the home-government pursued a policy, after the subjugation of New Spain, diametrically opposite to that suggested and advised by Cortés and the conquerors.

Of little avail were the entreaties of those who had the prosperity of Mexico at heart, and would have brought out the latent energies of her people. They were not allowed to encourage any industries which would conflict with those of Spain.

REAL ESTATE IN MEXICO.

It is as true now as twenty years ago, when Sartorius (a German by birth, a keen observer, and long a resident in Mexico), wrote, that the soil of the Republic of Mexico is, for the most part, in the hands of private individuals and corporations; comparatively little is State property, and this little chiefly in the northern districts. Mexico is a conquered country; the original conquerors selected large estates, and were confirmed in the possession of the same by the Spanish government. The original Indian possessors were included in these grants, as serfs; but they were suffered to retain the soil they cultivated, on paying rent. Subsequently a law was promulgated for the protection of the Indians, that the country round each village, to the distance of six hundred yards, measured from the church, should belong to the community. Many villages and towns which had fought as allies against the Aztecs, not only retained their lands, but were even rewarded with the confiscated lands of their neighbors. Churches and convents were endowed with landed estates, and whenever a spot was discovered without an owner, some Spanish official, soldier, or priest, soon managed to obtain it as a fief. The soil being thus partitioned out, it was natural for large estates to become the property of individuals, especially in the northern, less populous provinces, where the conquest gradually proceeded, and the leaders had leisure to acquire the conquered lands for themselves and their followers. The large estates in Mexico are *haciendas*, which, when intended for agriculture, are called *haciendas de labor*, and when for cattle-breeding, *haciendas de ganado*.

The agriculturists and graziers of Mexico belong by descent to the Creoles and Mestizos, and are its most independent class. "They are," continues Sartorius, "conservative, attached to old habits, to patriarchal customs, to discipline and order in the house, religious, honest, and hospitable, but at the same time frugal."

SEED-TIME AND HARVEST.

In some states, as Vera Cruz, Oaxaca, Tabasco, Guerrero, Jalisco, and Mexico, three harvests may be annually secured. The yield varies from a return of forty for one planted, to three hundred; but the general return is about a hundred and fifty for one. In the hot climate of the coast and in some portions of the interior seeds and grains may be kept from eight to ten months, in the temperate region from eighteen months to two years, and in the cold regions as long as four years.

The rainy season commences early in June, and lasts until the autumnal equinox. Frosts are frequent on the northern frontier in winter, and in other localities of great elevation. Hailstorms also occur in the colder regions, but not with frequency. Throughout the country it is more necessary to guard against drouth than excessive wet. Irrigation is needed, and largely used when practicable, all over the country. Should the rainy season be greatly retarded, the crops suffer, and are sometimes entirely lost. The hour of work in the hot climates are, for a day laborer, from five in the morning to eleven, and from three in the afternoon till seven; in the temperate and cold regions they are from morning to evening twilight, with two to three hours' rest for breakfast and dinner; on some haciendas the laborers have daily tasks which they complete at their discretion. The workmen are paid weekly, every Saturday evening or Sunday morning. The men received, before the late advent of railways raised the wages in the districts through which they run, from twenty-five to thirty-seven cents (with or without rations); and boys from twelve to eighteen. Women are rarely, though occasionally, employed in the fields, but prepare and carry to the laborers their meals. A ration (*racion*) consists of corn (*maiz*), beans (*frijoles*), salt, and *chile*, or red pepper, in sufficient quantity.

AGRICULTURE ON THE TABLE-LAND.

Sartorius, to whom we again refer as the best authority on the agriculture of Mexico, and one commended by Mexicans of high standing, has the following on this subject: The immense plateaux extending from the sixteenth to the thirtieth degrees of north latitude, which are from five thousand to eight thousand feet above the sea, produce nowhere tropical plants. The plants of the Old World are here met with, and maize, maguey, and the cactus for breeding the cochineal.

The husbandmen either resort to artificial irrigation or sow during the rainy season. In the beautiful valleys of Chiapes and Oaxaca, Perote, Puebla, Atlisco, Tlascala, Mexico, and Toluca, in the rich lowlands of Rio Grande de Santiago, and in many plains of the northern States, the rivers and brooks, sometimes even the lakes, are employed for artificial irrigation; and, when this does not suffice, by means of immense dikes elevated valleys have been converted into lakes, which fill during the rainy season, and supply the fields afterwards with necessary moisture. Many haciendas are furnished with expensive aqueducts which frequently convey the water for miles. All these estates grow wheat and maize, but on a larger scale than most European estates. The soil is plowed for wheat in October, the grain is sowed in November, and the water admitted to the furrows. The seed soon shoots up, is watered twice more during the winter, twice in spring, and ripens in May, or June.

The threshing is performed by means of horses or mules, treading out the grain, in the immediate vicinity of the fields. Many of the estates have their own mills, and send the flour to the towns, where the consumption of fine bread is greater in proportion than in Europe, while the native population of the villages consume chiefly maize bread, *tortilla.* Rye is cultivated here and there, oats nowhere, but barley to a considerable extent. Various sorts of maize are grown, which are, doubtless, varieties of one species, but must be selected according to climate and soil. If, as is occasionally the case, the early crop of maize suffers from the cold, barley is planted in the rainy season to make up for it, by which means the forage keeps down in price; for barley, with the exception of the small quantity lately required for brewing (now rapidly increasing) is used exclusively for feeding. Of the summer plants grown on the estates none are so universal as beans, which are in great request throughout the country. To these may be added horse beans, lentils, pistachios, chile (*capsicum annum*), batate or sweet potato, and occasionally rape and the potato. Vine cultivation is increasing in the north. The plateaux are rich in numerous species of cactus, which nature produces in the strangest forms.

The soil is rarely manured, the mineral components being such that their decomposition by air and water causes extraordinary fertility, and is constantly renewed. Many districts have been sown every year for centuries with maize, a plant that exhausts the soil more than any other, and still one constantly sees rich crops. If we regard the plants of Tlascala, Cholula, Toluca, and others, we find the soil covered with decomposed volcanic matter, or ashes and lava, which by gradual decomposition maintain its fertility. In many districts less favored by nature, the soil is lightly manured by flocks of sheep and goats. The manure from the stables of horses and mules is heaped up in the yard as rubbish, and in autumn burnt. Only horses and mules, such as are required for immediate use, are kept in stables, while horned cattle never have shelter. Their forage is almost always dry chopped straw, mixed with maize or barley, while the oxen sometimes get maize straw, and in the rainy season green fodder, besides the grass of the pasture, which is insufficient during the working season. With rare exceptions, oxen are used for ploughing; large estates often require two hundred yoke or more. The plow is still the ancient Roman one used in Spain, which merely furrows the soil, instead of turning it up. The harrow is not much used, a thorn-bush replacing it.

It is only during the maize harvest that the Indian women are actively employed in the field, it being considered more as a holiday, as all wish to be in at the *viuda* (the widow), the last ear that comes from the field. A tall stalk with the finest fruit is selected, ornamented with ribbons and plumes, and conveyed in triumphant procession to the master's house, as an indication of the harvest being completed. A dance, or at least some bottles of brandy, reward the attention of the servants. On all the haciendas the work is performed by day laborers, who live on the estate, and serve voluntarily. They are not boarded, but receive their pay in money, and usually every week a ration of maize and pulse. Should they be hindered from working by sickness, or if the master makes special advances for weddings, christenings, or burials, they are forced to incur debt, and are naturally obliged to work it off. The wages on the plateaux, about two *reales*, or twenty-five cents, are doubled and trebled on the coast. During harvest-time laborers are procured from the Indian villages, who come for a week or fortnight, with their provisions and tools, and are usually conducted by a *capitan*, appointed by the village alcade. These people are willing, moderate, and enduring, but are only to be obtained when they have finished harvesting in their own little plantations. The land belonging to most of the haciendas is too extensive for the proprietor to cultivate even the fourth part of it. He therefore devotes the remainder of it to cattle-breeding, or lets it out to farmers.

IN THE TIERRA CALIENTE, OR HOT COAST REGION.

"Agriculture on the table-lands," says the observant writer last quoted, and whom we shall follow a little farther, "has its prescribed limits, according to the soil and the climate. The European may easily fancy himself in his own country; the cornfields, the meadows, and market gardens, even the orchards, are those of temperate zones. On crossing the mountain ridges which encircle the plateaux, be it to the east or west, the whole physiognomy of the country assumes a decided tropical appearance; the heights are wooded; instead of the fine short Alpine grass, the plains are covered with taller grasses; the ground is overshadowed with creeping plants and brushwood; and agriculture obtains produce of a very different kind. The estates of the east coast differ from those of the west coast. In the latter all the perennial plants require artificial irrigation, whilst the coast lands of the Gulf, near the mountains, have rain throughout the year. Maize, *frijoles*, tobacco, rice, cotton, and indigo are cultivated as summer plants, that is to say, at the commencement of the rainy season, and require no further irrigation; the sugar-cane, coffee, cocoa, vanilla, rice, manioc, and the banana, must have irrigable land on the west side; on the east side in a few places only.

"On the table-land the soil must be plowed for sowing; in the *tierra caliente* the plow is met with on the larger plantations only. The rancheros plant their summer produce mostly in forest land, where no plow can be employed. In the dry season they hew down all the trees and bushes. The wood is allowed to dry for some months, and then set fire to. When the rain sets in, the grain is sown without the soil being turned up. With an iron-pointed stick holes are bored in the ground, and the seed-corn cast in. Maize, beans, rice, cotton, etc., are sown in this manner, and tobacco transplanted. In a few days the young seed shoots up, and with it innumerable weeds. Cotton thrives there only where the winter months are without rain, especially on the southern and ocean coasts, and on the west side of the Cordilleras to the height of three thousand feet. On the east side the winter in the neighborhood of the mountains is too damp. The cotton is spoiled by dew and rain, in consequence of which it is planted in the hot coast regions only.

"The indolence of the inhabitants is wonderful. A few dozen bananas, a small field with manioc and maize, afford nourishment without much labor. The coast rivers abound in excellent fish and turtle, and there are whole forests of palms affording palm-wine and oil. The small planter, or ranchero, of the warmer districts, besides his maize field, has usually some plots of land with beans, chile, tomatoes, yams, and bananas, which furnish him with a quantity of nourishment. The edible arum root bears from ten to fifteen pounds' weight of bulbs to each plant, the yam (*dioscorea*) develops monstrous roots weighing from fifty to eighty pounds, the *batata*, or sweet potato, produces its mealy bulb three or four months after being planted, and the manioc (*Jatropha manihot*) gives a quantity of excellent starch, while the bananas and plantain yield more fruit (upon which alone the family could subsist) than they can consume.

"The rancheros of the *tierra caliente* live mostly in frail huts of bamboo and reeds, open for the passage of cool breezes, and shaded by bananas and plantains. Beneath the roof swings a hammock, and very few, indeed, are the domestic utensils. They can seldom read or write. When they intend marrying, they must know part of the Catechism by heart, therefore, when the time comes, be crammed up to the mark. They are not fond of hard work, nor have they any need of it, as they have plenty to live upon if they devote but a few hours a day to agricultural labor. They are good hunters, know the haunts of the deer and wild boar, and track the wild turkey. The men tan the deer-skins remarkably well, dye and make their clothes of them; the women spin and weave cotton. During half the year there is little or nothing to be done in the field. The chase is then attended to, or the fibres of the long-leaved *bromelia pita*, or of the maguey, are prepared, cordage and ropes made of it, and sent to market. In other localities they collect copal, storax, and Peruvian balsam, the fruits of the oil-palm, pimento or vanilla. Many days, however, are passed extended on the mat, playing the guitar, sleeping, or staring up at the blue sky." To counterbalance the many advantages of life in the *tierra caliente*, there are the many dangers attending it, especially to the unacclimated, resulting from noxious disease peculiar to the tropic coast, the poisonous insects and reptiles, and the very monotony of an isolated existence.

HORSE AND CATTLE RAISING.

It is not owing solely to the fact that the large haciendas are too vast to cultivate, that so many Mexicans devote themselves to the herdsman's life. It is a pursuit of which they are fond, a love for which has been inherited, both by the Spaniard and the Mexican of the mixed race. The Indian rarely takes to the raising of cattle, horses, or sheep, both on account of poverty and natural disinclination. Cattle thrive best in the *tierra caliente*, while horses, sheep, and goats rarely do their best except in the upland region. In the case of the latter, the great number of prickly plants become entangled in their wool, and during the rainy season the humidity is such that the foot-rot and other diseases carry them off. The cattle are left entirely to nature, and seek their own pasture during the rainy season on the savannas, during the dry months in the shady forest. The different pasture-grounds of a hacienda are called *potreros*, and are under the care of herdsmen (*vaqueros*), each man having usually from five hundred to eight hundred head to look after. Although wild, the cattle do not shun man, and are easily attracted to the *vaquero* by means of salt, a bag of which he always carries at his saddle-bow.

All the Mexican cowherds are mounted, partly because it is impossible to survey such extensive tracts on foot, partly because they often require a fleet horse to catch stragglers. Frequently the animals injure themselves, the bulls fight, a sharp thorn, or a beast of prey (jaguar, puma, or wolf) wounds them, and, as in the hot regions, the flesh-fly lays its eggs in the wound, the assistance of the herdsman is indispensable. He therefore constantly has his lasso with him, made of leather or the fibres of the maguey. At full gallop he pursues the flying animal, casts the noose about its neck, quickly turns his horse's head, and drags the struggling prisoner to the nearest tree, to which it is soon bound. In a moment, he has dismounted, has cast a second noose about the hind-feet, and with one jerk the heaviest beast is extended on the ground; the hind and fore feet are quickly tied together, and now the surgical operation can be performed at leisure. The *vaquero* endures the hardest toil for very little pay, living a life of constant fatigue, and is in the saddle by night and by day. He always lives in the middle of his pasture-grounds, near a watering-place, and has a strong inclosure of stone or logs (*corral*), into which the herd can be driven. The calves are taken thither when some days old, and tied up under a shed. Instinct leads the cows twice a day to the enclosure to give their young the required nourishment. Part of the milk is withdrawn, and this is done more for the sake of taming both cow and calf, and to accustom them to man, than for the sake of the milk. After two months the calf is set at liberty, but it now remains, especially if it be driven once a week with the herd to receive a little salt.

Many estates there are, throughout Mexico, that possess from ten thousand to twenty thousand head of cattle, and it frequently happens that, owing to the difficulty of obtaining herdsmen, whole herds run wild, and are not readily caught. It is indispensable in the raising of cattle that they be driven into corral at least once a year, and must often be treated to salt. The yearly branding of calves and cattle is called *herradero*, and is made an important festival. The great profit is in the sale of the oxen and old cows to the butchers, as a great quantity of meat is consumed in the country. The ranchero usually slaughters his fat cattle himself, and makes *sesina* or *tasajo* of the meat. This is done by cutting all the flesh into strips about four inches broad and two thick and several feet in length. It is then well sprinkled with fine salt, and with the juice of lemons, the whole mass being wrapped up over night in the hide. The next day, as soon as the sun is high enough, the strips are hung upon lines, and thoroughly dried by the air and sun. The process is finished in some days, and the meat is then packed in bales, and sent to market.

Vast quantities of this dried meat are consumed, for it is savory, keeps well, and is soon prepared, it being only necessary to lay a piece on the coals and roast it.

In the shrubless plains of Zacatecas, San Luis Potosi, Durango, Coahuila, and Chihuahua, continues the authority upon whom we are mainly depending for this information, the soil is everywhere poorly manured. In the rainy season, from June till October, these plains are covered with tall grass, but in December all begins to fade, the pools in the hollow dry up, and in the warmest months, April and May, water is frequently not met with for days. In these deserts the horses and mules are chiefly bred. The haciendas are seldom sufficiently furnished with water, and are forced to have recourse to tanks, in which it is collected, or to bore deep wells.

It is infinitely more difficult to breed horses than cattle. The latter are impelled by instinct to seek for watering-places, which they find in the deepest ravines, often wandering several leagues a day to a river or lake, and always returning before night to the favorite pasture. The horses, on the contrary, must be driven every day to water, as they would otherwise die of thirst. The mares always keep together in troops of forty or sixty (in *atajos*) being led by a stallion, who often trots round the troop to hurry those that lag behind, and who fights furiously with any other stallion that may chance to approach.

The herdsmen of these troops are the boldest horsemen in existence. They lead a poor life, as their salary rarely exceeds five dollars a month ; they live in wretched huts, and seldom behold a village, or enjoy the pleasure of society. Half their time is passed in the saddle, and their delight is to race with other herdsmen, to cast the lasso, and to mount the untamed horses and mules.

Good stallions are dear, and command high prices. Mules are bred on the northern plateaux, and require more attention than horses. Four-year fillies are bought up from the pasture at from eight to ten dollars each, mules from twenty-five to thirty dollars. The large estates have often from eight thousand to ten thousand horses and mules, and usually effect their sales in winter, in the larger towns.

Sheep-breeding is carried on, in most districts, less for the wool than for the tallow and flesh. The race is bad, and the wool inferior, although the extensive dry pastures, the mountain-ridges covered with aromatic herbs, and the equable climate, would be in the highest degree favorable to an improved breed. From egotism and petty jealousy, the Spaniards never introduced the Merino breed to the colonies. It is on record, however, that Cortez was the first to do this very thing, after he had secured the estate and marquisate of Oaxaca. Just as they prohibited the culture of the vine, of olives, and mulberries in Mexico, in order to retain for the mother-country the trade in wine, oil, and silk, so were they determined to keep the trade in fine cloth in their own hands, without reflecting that the traffic in fine wool would have brought them in a far more considerable profit. In recent years, however, some of the more enterprising Mexicans have procured superior ewes and rams from Saxony and the Pyrenees, and the effect is already becoming apparent. Towards the end of the rainy season the flocks are collected, the fat wethers and old ewes selected and slaughtered, and the flesh stewed down in a range of large coppers. The firm tallow, in masses of about two hundred pounds, is packed in sheep skins, and forwarded to the cities and mining districts, where it meets with a ready sale. The slaughtering period (*matanza*) usually lasts a month, and is a holiday for the shepherds who have only to perform the slaughtering, skinning, and cutting up, receiving as extra wages the heads and intestines of the victims, and fatten themselves and families for a long time with heads and livers. The cooked meat from which the fat has been extracted (*carne de chito*) lies there in complete mountains after a *matanza;* it is bought up by dealers, and sold in the villages.

Goats and swine are also reared in great numbers, both, also, for the sake of their fat. The steep, craggy hills and mountains, covered with thorns and creeping-plants, afford them a perfect paradise, where they are fattened with greater celerity than in the slums of great cities. The milk either of goat or cow is not utilized to any extent in Mexico; as a consequence, butter is scarce, and cheese mostly imported. The chief profit of goats is in the tallow, a fat he-goat yielding about twelve, and a she-goat ten pounds of tallow. In Jalisco and Michoacan many estates fatten a thousand swine annually, and sell them in droves to the soap-boilers and ham-salters of Toluca and Perote.

IRRIGATION.

By the establishing of a school of agriculture, and by the encouraging of farmers to procure the best breeds of cattle, etc., the "Department of Public Works," in Mexico, has in mind the thorough cultivation of Mexican soil, by the best and most improved processes.

It offers some inducements to immigrants, but prefers those of the Latin race, as more readily assimilating with the native population. But its attention should rather be directed towards a system of irrigation, which, by a network of arteries, or by means of artesian wells, should feed the vast deserted tracks with water,— that life-blood of agriculture. The native Indians once possessed extensive irrigating works, but they were destroyed by the Spaniards, who, in addition to this, eventually deprived the high valleys and plateaux of their forest coverings; and the soil, thus exposed to a tropical sun, without protection of undergrowth or timber, was carried away by descending torrents. This is the condition of the great Valley of Mexico, whose surrounding hills are almost entirely denuded of soil as well as of vegetation. The great success resulting from irrigation, in California, New Mexico, and other portions of the lost territory of Mexico, should remind the Mexicans of the great prestige of their ancestors, and incite them to the re-building of ancient *acequias* and canals, under the care of the State.

"If all the country," says Señor Cubas, "were populated, even in proportion to Guanajuato, the census of the Republic would reach 58,000,000, and then agricultural products would be so much greater that they would constitute an element of enormous wealth." Within the territory, at present, there are more than 5,700 haciendas, and 13,800 ranchos; the value of landed property, based simply on its valuation for taxes, was, in 1876, $176,397,300, without taking into account streams, grazing-lands, orchards, and other rural property.

These estimates are taken from the great government report of Mexico, — *Estadistica de la Republica Mexicana,* — which has been the basis of the preceding article, and which we have every reason to believe approximately accurate. From the same source we also obtain the

AGRICULTURAL PRODUCTIONS FOR THE YEAR 1880.

	KILOGRAMS.	VALUE.
Chickling vetch	12,650,460	$543,283
Cotton	25,177,760	6,605,831
Beneseed (*sesamum orientale*)	3,050,140	153,643
Canary seed	1,121,375	57,410
Anise	1,175,950	127,268
Indigo	192,246	358,002
Rice	15,166,588	1,248,244
Sugar	70,090,550	8,761,317
Cacao	1,443,002	1,140,050
Coffee	7,961,808	2,060,382
Barley	232,334,023	4,403,742
Cumin seed	102,337	23,500
Capsicum	54,128,140	4,196,482
Beans	210,188,526	8,406,211
Chick peas	11,485,422	471,075
Beans (garden)	15,722,561	477,610
Sisal hemp	40,080,000	3,352,000
Aloe fibre (*ixtle*)	2,231,890	154,053
Lentil	2,102,625	83,043
Maize	5,309,563,939	112,164,424
Potatoes	10,557,738	457,592
Straw	196,245,600	1,962,879
Tobacco	7,504,990	2,006,153
Wheat	338,704,093	17,436,345
Vanilla	55,118	651,938
Sarsaparilla	488,022	149,489
Total	6,569,524,903	$177,451,986

ANNUAL MOVEMENT OF AGRICULTURAL INDUSTRIES.

Olive oil	24,815	$27,629
Rapeseed oil	434,400	278,292
Beneseed oil	216,300	156,277
Linseed oil	608,798	317,734
Brandy	531,576	114,453
Rum	19,317,608	2,052,150
Beer	10,058,636	768,703
Flour	124,057,653	13,463,833
Chocolate	671,278	731,367
Sacks, ropes, etc.	835,277	222,702
Various articles	1,868,048	433,526
Maguey liquor	9,016,000	1,176,000
Maguey wine	5,152,764	570,646
Straw and palm-leaf hats and other fabrics	745,449	370,730
Ordinary pulque	76,430,097	323,232
Fine pulque	100,213,127	3,935,995
Common pulque	10,511,073	330,301
White wine	2,212,209	1,154,196
Red wine	3,529,718	1,508,475
Various liquors	2,144,255	941,021
Coco wine	131,985	34,341
Palm wine	589,467	51,258
Total	369,300,533	$28,962,861

SOME SPECIAL PRODUCTS.

"The merciful hand of Providence," says Lemprière ("Notes on Mexico," 1862), "has bestowed on the Mexicans a magnificent land, abounding in resources of all kinds, — a land where none ought to be poor, and where misery ought to be unknown, — a land whose products and riches of every kind are abundant, and as varied as they are rich. It is a country endowed to profusion with every gift that man can desire or envy; all the metals from gold to lead; every sort of climate from perpetual snow to tropical heat, and inconceivable fertility."

In order to indicate the vast range of food and industrial plants found in Mexico, the writer has selected some of the more important, — mainly tropical productions, — which are presented as worthy of attention. They are arranged in alphabetical order: —

Arrowroot, from both species, *Maranta arundinacea*, and *Tacca pinnatifida*, finds in certain sections of Mexico, a soil and climate adapted to its successful production. The first-mentioned species, a native of South America, may have been cultivated by the aborigines of Central America. In the West Indies, in some islands, great attention is paid to its cultivation, with good results. Although not an object of much attention in Mexico, it should form an important article of export, and is herewith recommended to the agriculturists of the *tierra caliente*.

Banana and *Plantain*, *Musa sapientum* and *Musa paradisiaca*. — Everywhere in the hot coast region, and on the lower borders of "the temperate land," wherever cultivation is carried on, may be seen the banana and its sister-plant, the plantain. The first, sweet, luscious, and equally good raw or cooked, is not, perhaps, more valuable than the second, which forms the tropical aborigines' staple article of diet. There is little reason to doubt that the plantain is indigenous to tropical America, and was cultivated by the aboriginal inhabitants long before the coming of Columbus. The many varieties of the banana are the result of long cultivation, and the successful introduction into America of plants from Africa and China. Regarding its productiveness, we may repeat that oft-quoted statement of Humboldt, that thirty-three pounds of wheat and ninety-nine pounds of potatoes, require the same space of ground to grow upon, as will produce four thousand pounds of bananas. From a year to eighteen months is required to ripen the fruit from the first planting, but as suckers spring up all about the original stock, there is afterwards no labor, except that of gathering the immense bunches of fruit, some of which attain to eighty pounds weight. These plants, like the agave and coco-palm, are useful to man in many ways; for besides producing delicious fruit, they furnish material, from stalk and leaves, for paper, cordage, etc.

It is said that the first banana was brought into America by a Dominican, in 1516, from the Canaries to Haiti, from whence it was transplanted to the Continent. The name *Plátano*, of the Spanish, is supposed to be derived from *Palan*, its most ancient name; *Banana*, the French, from its native Guinea appellation, and *Musa*, the Italian, is taken from the Arabic.

Barley, Spanish *cebada*, introduced by the Spaniards, growing in the cold region, or *tierra fria*, to a higher altitude than maize, though now used principally as fodder, in a green state, it will undoubtedly attain to great importance in the brewing industries of the Republic, and as an article of food. The estimated value of its production in 1880, was above $400,000, constantly increasing. This most ancient of all grains, and the most hardy, which has been found in the lake-dwellings of Switzerland, in deposits belonging to the stone-period, was not in cultivation (so far as is known), among the Aztecs.

Beans and Chile. — Mexico has not a monopoly of these products, though their consumption is enormous, the first (*frijoles*) constituting the chief aliment of the poorer classes, next to corn, and the latter, *chile* (*Capsicum annuum*), an invariable accompaniment. Of the first, Mexico is estimated to have produced, in 1880, over 200 kilograms, worth $8,406,211; and of chile, $4,196,482.

Cacao, Theobroma cacao. — The tree producing the *cacao*, or chocolate-bean, flourishes in the humid climate of the *tierra caliente*, especially in the State of Tabasco, and produces an important article of export. The production in 1879, based on information received by the bureau of statistics in Mexico, was of the value of over a million dollars. The tree, which requires shade as well as moisture, in its early years, yields fruit at about the same age as the orange. Its cultivation is simple, and the preparation of the seed for export, requires little labor, though watchful care is necessary.

Cactaceæ. — As Mexico belongs to the botanical region of the cacti and peppers, it is not strange that we find here the cactus family flourishing in greatest vigor. Of the five hundred species found in America, Mexico has her full share, and they form, sometimes, the only vegetation of certain vast plains, which without them would be level wastes, without an object to relieve the eye. Some of them, as the *Cerei*, rise to the height of sixty feet, their straight, rigid, and spiny trunks supporting great branches like candelabra, whence their name, candelabra cacti; others creep along the ground. The great, globular echinocacti frequently attain to a weight of two hundred pounds. All produce brilliant flowers; all are covered with spines, and are strangely grotesque in shape. The cochineal cactus (described in "Travels in Mexico," p. 529) was formerly of great value; but, since the discovery of analine dyes, the culture of cochineal has almost entirely ceased. Besides the edible fruits yielded by several species, as the *opuntia*, the *nopal*, etc., the *cactaceæ* minister to man in many indirect ways. The nopal figures prominently in Mexican history, for it was upon a cactus (nopal), that the Aztecs beheld their traditional eagle perched, when they at last reached Tenochtitlan, and it may be seen emblazoned on the national banner of the Mexicans, and stamped on all their coins. The giant Betahaya supplies in the north the place of the *organo*, or organ cactus in the south.

Cassava (*Jatropha manihot* and *Jatropha janipha*), *mandioca*, or *manioc*, a plant of tropical America long in use by the native inhabitants. Of these two species one, *Jatropha manihot*, is a deadly poison if eaten in the green state, but if the juice is evaporated by exposure to the sun, or artificial heat, may be eaten with impunity. The tubers require a dry soil not much elevated, and ripen in about eight months from time of planting, which is done by cuttings. The cassava, or native bread, is prepared by peeling off the dark outer rind, grinding the roots after a thorough washing, and baking the "farine" in thin cakes over a hot fire. Tapioca is prepared from it; the tuber is rich in starch.

Chirimoya (*Anona tripetala*), an American fruit, said to surpass in flavor any grown in Europe. A native of Peru, but grown in Mexico, attaining to large size. This fruit is heart-shaped, the rind green, covered with small tubercles, and inclosing a snow-white, juicy pulp, filled with black kernels. One writer calls it a "masterpiece of nature;" another declares that its taste is quite incomparable. Both fruit and blossoms exhale a most delightful odor.

Coca (the *Erythroxylon coca*), a narcotic and stimulant plant, the leaves of which are used by the natives of Brazil, Bolivia, and Peru. Its home is in the sultry valleys of the eastern slopes of the Peruvian and Bolivian Andes. The shrub bears a foliage of lustrous green and white flowers ripening into small scarlet berries. When the leaves are brittle enough to break upon being bent, they are stripped from the plant, dried in the sun, and packed in sacks. Coca lessens the desire for food, and bestows upon the person using it in moderate quantities great powers of endurance. Especially is it valuable in the ascent of great elevations, preventing the difficulty of respiration. The writer has used it with apparently good effect in an ascent of Popocatapetl, in 1881, when he easily climbed to the peak of that mighty volcano, experiencing but little uneasiness from the rarefaction of the atmosphere. No record exists of its first discovery, but it was in use in the temples of the Incas, when Pizarro invaded Peru, and the priests chewed coca while performing their rites. It is estimated that 30,000,000 pounds of the dried leaf are annually consumed; and it has been suggested that its use be more widely extended as a substitute for tea and coffee. There is no reason why coca should not be successfully grown on the slopes of the Mexican mountains, where climate, altitude, and all the conditions of growth can be found in perfection.

The Coco-palm. — To the dweller in the coast country of Mexico, there is no more valuable product, be it tree or vegetable, than the coco-palm, *cocos nucifera*. There is always danger of confusion in speaking of three totally dissimilar products: the cacao, coca, and cocoa. The true spelling of this word should be without the terminal letter, a. Coco: its Latin name is *cocos*, its Spanish, *coco*, and its French, also. The late Charles Kingsley used this orthography, and there is little doubt that *cocoa* is wrong, and a corruption of cacao, which is the name of the *Theobroma cacao*. In order to avoid confusion, we shall speak of it by its correct appellation, *coco*.

It is ever found growing by the sea, loving salt water and salt sea-breezes more than the perfumed gales from out the mountain valleys.

It may be seen drooping over a beach of golden sand, and forming a living barrier between beach and cultivated land, or dotting the valleys, or standing up lone and ragged upon a wind-swept promontory; but it is almost within sound of the surf-beat of the waves. It may stray away towards the mountains, may climb a few hills, and may shelter a little village of huts beneath the waving crowns of itself and companions at some distance from the sea; but in its luxuriance and beauty and profusion it is only found near the coast. Other palms replace it in the mountains; other palms wander far away, and revel in shade and moisture and cool breezes; but this palm, as if ever mindful of the restless waves that bore its parent nut to these shores, delights to keep them company. And the coco loves man, delighting in the proximity of habitations and cultivated fields. Do you meet with a negro hut, alone or with others clustered about it, no matter how humble, dilapidated, obscure, above it droops the feathery crown of a palm, its leaves caressing it, its nuts hanging in abundance ready to drop at the will of the owner.

Broad valleys stretch along the shore, extending far back into the hills, one waving sea of yellow cane, with no object to relieve the billowy plain but the coco-palm and its more aspiring brother, the towering palmiste. About the sugar-house and the dwelling of the owner and the overseer, it is scattered in picturesque groups. The coco is to the tropics what the pine is to the North, the elm to New England, the magnolia to the South.

Coffee. — First found in the forests of Abyssinia, beneath the tropic sun of Africa, coffee was not known to the world beyond till about four hundred years ago. Its cultivation was then confined to a small Arabian province, but its high value induced the Dutch to introduce it into Java, in 1690, and as a rare plant into the botanical gardens of Amsterdam. The New World obtained its supply from a single plant, which a French naval officer carried to Martinique, in the West Indies, in 1720, depriving himself of water, when parching with thirst, that the tender shoot might survive. From this one tree, it is said, all the American tropical colonies obtained their seed, which has multiplied to such an extent that Brazil, the West Indies, and Mexico supply us with as much as Java and Ceylon. These are at present the great coffee countries, the product of Mocha being small in quantity.

It is at an elevation of about four thousand feet that the coffee best thrives, for here it gets shade and moisture, — which the lowlands cannot invariably supply, — and a temperature changing but slightly from year to year. When a grove is started in the primitive forest, many of the large trees are left standing to give the required shade; and when commenced on the low lands where there are no trees, broad-leaved plants, like the banana, are planted by its side to protect from the sun. The tree naturally attains a height of about twenty feet, but in the plantations is pruned down, forming with its straight, horizontal branches a beautiful dome-shaped mass of green. The leaves are broad and glossy green, sometimes concealing the "berries," or fruit, which cluster along the slender twigs and branches. The coffee is shaped like a small bean, and two of these beans are found side by side, adhering by their flat surface, enclosed in a pulp covered by an outside skin, forming a berry the size of a cherry. This is at first green, but ripens into a bright red when it is gathered.

A coffee-plantation in these upland valleys is one of the most beautiful things out of doors. Wide straight paths are opened through it, above which are the dark-green coffee-trees gleaming with berries, or filling the air with perfumed gales from clouds of snowy blossoms.

If there is one production over another that has especial value in Mexico, it is the coffee. Nowhere in the United States can it be successfully raised, there being no suitable combination of soil, climate, and *altitude*, for its perfect growth. The range of the coffee-plant extends only between the isothermals of 25° north and 30° south of the equator, and it cannot be successfully grown in places where the temperature is ever below 55°. Hence this leaves the United States out in the cold, and gives, in the Western Hemisphere, Mexico, the West Indies, and a great portion of South America, exclusive control of coffee-cultivation.

"When grown at the extremes of climate, it is small, generally much lighter, and the actual number of berries is far less than that grown in a genial climate. Experience has proved that from latitute 6° to 12° an elevation of from three thousand to four thousand feet is the most suited, whilst beyond this, five hundred feet of elevation should be allowed for every degree of latitude." Difference in locality of production has little to do with the flavor of coffee, notwithstanding a general belief to the contrary. In Mexico, for instance, the coffee of Colima and Michoacan is declared to surpass that of Cordova and Tabasco; but this superiority, if it exists, is owing to better preparation for the market, or curing, and perhaps to a more thorough cultivation. The quantity of rain, says one writer, is found to exercise a material effect upon the quality of the crop, and a dry climate produces a better flavored and more "colory" bean than that where excessive moisture prevails.

The coffee-tree, says the same authority, flourishes in hilly districts, where its roots can be kept dry, while its leaves are refreshed with frequent showers.

"Rocky ground, with rich, decomposed mould in the fissures, agrees best with it. Though it would grow to the height of fifteen or twenty feet, yet it is usually kept down by pruning to that of five feet, for increasing its productiveness, as well as for the convenience of cropping. It begins to yield the third year, but is not generally in full bearing until the fifth. In coffee husbandry, the plants should be placed eight feet apart, as the trees throw out extensive horizontal branches." The berry must not be picked till fully ripe, then dried in the sun, with the pulp and parchment attached, then passed between wooden rollers, or brayed in a mortar, to remove the dried envelope, and winnowed.

The coffee-plants should be first started in a nursery, whence they are transplanted to the ground assigned for the grove, and during their early years protected from the heat of the sun by bananas and plantains.

Coffee improves in aroma by keeping, and although it loses in weight, it gains in color, and quality. Most of the Mexican coffee is sold direct from the plantations, and is not allowed to arrive at that perfect state acquired by the "Old Government" Java, which possesses a spicy aroma the light-colored berries do not.

In the opening years of this century, coffee was not very extensively cultivated in Brazil, but that country supplies to the United States the greatest proportion used. "The first cargo of coffee from Brazil entered at the port of Salem, Mass., and consisted of 1,522 bags. In 1871, the United States consumed 316,609,765 pounds of coffee, 244,809,600 pounds of which came from Brazil, 27,776,000 from Java, Sumatra, etc., and but 6,728,165 from Central American, Mexican, and other foreign ports." In 1874, according to the Consular Report, the value of coffee exported from Mexico to the United States was $543,352; the amount of coffee exported from Vera Cruz. to all ports in 1876, was $1,146,845. For the year ending 1880, the total value of coffee export from Mexico, was $2,060,382. To show the great value of the coffee crop to us, and to illustrate the growth of this special industry, the following figures are appended, obtained from the United States consulate in Vera Cruz. Total amount of coffee exported from Mexico to the United States only, from March 31, 1876, to March 31, 1881:—

Year ending March 31, 1877	$660,685 82
Year ending March 31, 1878	1,320,612 58
Year ending March 31, 1879	1,064,862 17
Year ending March 31, 1880	1,490,171 87
Year ending March 31, 1881	1,289,716 16

All the coast states of Southern Mexico, on both the Gulf and Pacific, have excellent soil and climate for the growing of coffee; but the most accessible are the Eastern, and the coffee region of Vera Cruz is the best known, while portions of Colima and Michoacan may contain the most favored combinations for success.

Coffee will certainly form the most remunerative of Mexico's agricultural products, as there is a vast area especially adapted to its culture, which lies adjacent to ports connected by short steam-lines with the United States, and penetrated by the great railroads running southward.

Cotton. — Spanish *Algodon*, from Arabic *Algoton*, indigenous plant of Mexico, found there by the Spaniards. Indians clothed with cotton garments were first seen by Columbus, near the mainland, off the east coast of Yucatan, in 1502, nearly two thousand years after the first mention of cotton fibre by Herodotus. Traditions are not lacking as to the ancient use of cotton by the Toltecs and the Aztecs, the date even of the adoption by the latter tribe of cotton garments in place of those of skin, being entered in their annals. As to the Toltecs, it was entered in their sacred book that Quetzalcoatl, god of the air, grew cotton of all colors in his gardens, and taught them its many uses. Cotton garments, quilted armor of cotton, and beautiful mantles were woven by the Indians of the plateaux from this fibre. The breastplates of cotton were proof against Indian arrows, and were finally adopted by the conquerors themselves, while many articles of apparel were often woven of a fineness and almost lustre of silk. In cotton and cacao seeds the inhabitants of the lowlands, such as had not gold and precious stones, paid their tribute to the Aztec rulers. Throughout the Republic of Mexico, there were, even as at the present day, primitive looms, and the manufacture of cotton goods was among the first industries, in point of time, as it is now in importance, in that country.

The original home of cotton being in the tropical zone, no one can say that this is not another plant native to the soil of Mexico, and which, like maize, may have started from this point, and have been carried north and south. Although it is within the century past that cotton has acquired importance in the manufactures of the world, yet we know that the aboriginal inhabitants of tropical America, the more civilized of them, were acquainted with its uses at least five hundred years ago.

It is one of those plants, says Humboldt, of which the cultivation was as ancient among the Aztecs as that of the maize and the maguey. Cotton thrives only where the winter months are without rain, says Sartorius. The districts of Tlacotalpam, Cuzamalopan, and Tustla, in the State of Vera Cruz, and the coast of Yucatan, produce the best cotton on the east side. It is cultivated in only twelve States of the Republic, and the amount produced is not sufficient for home consumption, large quantities being imported from the United States. There is little doubt that vast tracts of uncultivated land exist which could be made to yield bountiful crops of cotton, such as the extensive plains of the south of Michoacan, the district of Mina, in Guerrero, the savannas of Vera Cruz, the extraordinarily fertile country about the laguna of Tlahualila, and the so-called desert region of Chihuahua. Every year increases the importance of cotton-raising in Mexico, especially in view of the fact that vast tracts of land hitherto inaccessible, and rendered unsafe through the presence of hostile Indians, are being opened to immigration by the railroads. Regarding the prospect of profitable results from engaging in cotton-raising, it would be difficult to advise, since skill, experience, and capital are required in this industry; but there is certainly a large demand for cotton, which it will take our railroads yet some years to satisfy.

Yucatan, Tabasco, Chiapas, Vera Cruz, and Durango are the principal cotton-growing states. To these Consul-General Strother, in his official report, adds Guerrero, Colima, Oaxaca, Chihuahua, Sinaloa, Sonora, Jalisco, Michoacan, and Coahuila.

The annual production of Coahuila he estimates at 3,000,000 pounds. "In the 'Laguna Country' cotton is perennial, and does not require to be planted oftener than once in ten years." This district, containing about 1,200,000 acres, lies partly in Coahuila and partly in Durango, is of extraordinary fertility, and well adapted to cotton, but is very little cultivated, and the cotton product is diminishing yearly. Durango's cotton crop he estimates at 4,000,000 pounds yearly, that of Sinaloa at 1,700,000 and of Sonora at 1,000,000 pounds. The cotton-belt of Mexico is not so well-defined as that of the United States, depending more upon altitude than latitude; but it is not so broad that cotton will ever become an important article of export. In fact, the best goods manufactured for Mexico are from cotton of the United States, imported at Vera Cruz from New Orleans, and, in some instances, transported on mule-back hundreds of miles into the interior.

And this is notwithstanding the enormous yield, in 1880, estimated at 25,177,760 kilograms, valued at $6,605,831.

Henequen, or *Sisal Hemp* (*Agave Sisalensis*.[1]) — From an official report published in Merida, capital of Yucatan, in 1876, it appears that the peninsula produced, in that year, fibre to the amount of 22,000,000 pounds, the largest part of which (about 18,000,000) was exported in the shape of hemp to New York, London, and New Orleans, and the rest shipped manufactured to Cuba and the Mexican ports. Taking one and a quarter pound of fibre as the average yearly production of each plant, it was estimated that there was at that time more than 18,000,000 plants under cultivation, keeping in operation over 420 scraping-wheels, moved by 229 steam-engines, with a total of 1,733 horse-power, and 30 wheels moved by animal power. Each wheel cleans daily, on an average, 300 pounds of fibre, working but half the year.

"For some time after the cultivation of hemp — henequen — was seriously undertaken by the planters of Yucatan (notwithstanding the invention of the 'fibre-cleaner,' and the cheapness of wages for laborers that obtained), the merchants of that section encountered many obstacles in introducing the staple in the markets of the world. "For the numberless farms of Russia still produced their vast quantities of that hemp from which is manufactured the stout cordage so highly esteemed by the mariners of the civilized world, while on the arid plains of India the Manila fibre, so highly rated for its flexibility and utility in the manufacture of rope for the running rigging of ships, flourished in luxuriant abundance, and to-day is the greatest rival of the Southern henequen.

"But in 1854 the war waged by France, England, and Sardinia against the empire of Russia terminated for some time the traffic in hemp, so important to that empire. The merchants and factors of Yucatan took advantage of this event to introduce their staple into the markets of Europe. It was utilized by the English and French in the manufacture of cordage and ropes, nor was it long before the discovery was made that the proportion of one-fourth Manila fibre with three-fourths henequen made excellent rope, sufficiently flexible for all practicable purposes, but at the same time considerably cheaper than cordage composed of Manila alone. Thus a great impetus was given to the culture of henequen in Yucatan. Thousands of acres of stony land, so sterile as to unfit it for the cultivation of corn or vegetables, were immediately utilized in the culture of Yucatan's only staple. Men who were looked upon as the unfortunate owners of leagues of desert wastes, by the planting of the henequen, in the course of six or seven years became wealthy personages, for each plant on their farms yielded them an income of ten cents per year, even when the price of the precious fibre ruled low. For some years after the Russian war the price of henequen averaged about seven cents per pound, while the principal

---

[1] See "Travels in Mexico," chap. iv.

markets where it was consumed were New York and Liverpool, Antwerp and Hamburg. But in 1872 the price of the staple fell, and fluttered from five cents to six and six and a quarter cents per pound. In 1878 the price dropped as low as four and a half cents per pound, and then the unhappy planters lamented their hard fate in the depreciation of a staple that paid them for its cultivation some ten or twelve per cent at this low price clear of all expenses on the value of their farms, as assessed by them when the price ruled as high as eight and nine cents per pound, and when they were gaining at least twenty-five per cent on the capital invested.

"Even now, when the price is from five and a half to six cents per pound, the cultivation of henequen is a most profitable investment for capital. Labor rules at from six to eight dollars per month, while the system of peonage that obtains in Yucatan is still more oppressive and more degrading even than in Mexico."

From statistics furnished the writer by United States Consul Aymé, at Merida, Yucatan, it will be seen that the henequen industry is assuming vast and unexpected proportions:—

Values to all places: 1880, $1,805,848.18; 1881, $2,774,166.88, increase over previous year, $969,318.70; 1882, $2,729,556.07, decrease from previous year, $44,610.81.

Bales to the United States: 1880, 85,434; 1881, 116,209; 1882, 109,867.

Bales to Europe: 1880, 11,917; 1881, 23,424; 1882, 25,216.

Three thousand bales were burned at Progreso in 1881, of which 2,481 were destined for the United States, and 519 for Europe. The noticeable features are, for three years: a great increase in exportations in 1881 over 1880; a considerable decrease in 1882 from 1881. But while the percentage of increase in number of bales in 1881 was about 40 per cent for the United States, the European imports were over 100 per cent greater, and in 1882 the whole decrease fell on the United States, while Europe increased her imports, still further lowering our amount.

Indigo, which was once a special product of Mexican soil, has declined in importance, like cochineal, until it is no longer profitable to engage in its cultivation. The total amount for 1880 is given at $358,000.

Cochineal, which was formerly raised and exported to the amount of over $2,000,000 annually, has no longer a value that will tempt the cultivator in Mexico other than the patient Indian, descendant of a long line of cochineal raisers, to attempt its difficult, though fascinating, culture. These two industries are very evidently relegated to the things of the past.

Maize and *Wheat.* — Indian corn, or maize, was probably the only cereal originally possessed by the Mexicans, but all the grains of Europe have been successfully introduced. Maize grows everywhere from coast to mountain-top; wheat and barley only in the colder regions: but all flourish here, and yield abundant harvests.

Columbus, in his first voyage, in 1492, discovered corn in use by the Indians of Cuba, and afterwards by those of Haiti. "Among the trophies of the New World that this great navigator laid at the feet of his sovereigns, on returning from this remarkable voyage to the unknown country, were a few ears of *maize,* or ' Indian corn.' Neglected were they amongst the mass of rich plunder — gold, gems, and strange copper-skinned captives — that greeted the eyes of Ferdinand and Isabella; but the golden ears were of far more value to the world than all the treasure that subsequently flowed into their coffers from New Spain."

The spread of the wonderful grain was rapid, and that which had hitherto constituted the chief food of the American Indian was soon all over Europe, Asia, and

Africa. A thousand years before our country acquired a name, the Indians of Mexico cultivated this precious cereal. At the present day, even, it is almost their sole support.

On the discovery of America by Europeans, says Humboldt, the *sea maiz* (*tlaolli* in the Aztec, *mahiz* in the Haytian) was cultivated from the most southern part of Chili to Pennsylvania (much farther north even than that).

Maize, or Indian corn, is certainly of tropical birth. Its broad, clinging leaves, its tall, tassel-crowned form, and luxuriant growth, all proclaim it as a native of the tropics. The home of the maize is undoubtedly the Mexican plateau. Either there or on the equally elevated plains of Peru, Indian corn had its birth. There it finds the necessary union of hot "growing" days with cool, moist nights.

In a journey through the Indian hill-towns of Southern Mexico, the writer has ridden for days through successive valleys filled with maize, where the villages were entirely hidden in vast fields, and where the great stalks with their waving tassels, like the feathered crests of warriors of old, reached the height of fifteen feet. Humboldt esteemed the cerealia of Mexico far ahead of that of Europe in point of productiveness, and Mr. Ward, British minister to Mexico, sixty years ago, wrote: "There are few parts, either of the *tierra caliente* or of the table-land, in which maize is not cultivated with success. In the low hot grounds upon the coast, and on the slope of the cordillera, its growth is more colossal than on the table-land; but even there, at 7,000 and 8,000 feet above the level of the sea, its fecundity is such as will hardly be credited in Europe."

The estimated product of maize in Mexico for the year ending 1880 was 5,309,563,939 kilograms; in value, $112,164,424.

The first wheat in Mexico was accidentally introduced, it is believed, in some rice brought with the stores of the Spanish army, and was first planted before 1530. From that humble beginning, the wheat crop of Mexico has steadily increased, until at the present day, this cereal finds congenial surroundings everywhere on the plateaus. The Mexican wheat, according to Humboldt, "is of the very best quality, and may be compared with the finest Andalusian grain." Regarding the yield, he further says, speaking of the principal great valleys of Mexico, "At Cholula, the common harvest is from 30 to 40, but frequently exceeds 70 to 80, for one. In the Valley of Mexico maize yields 200, and wheat 18 or 20 fold. In the northern part of Mexico, he estimated the return as lower; yet where irrigation is practised, as in California and Arizona, former provinces of New Spain, or Mexico, the result has been astonishing.

The estimated production for 1880, throughout Mexico, was 338,704,093 kilograms, valued at $17,436,345. Fine flour is ground in Mexico, but not equal to the American, which sells largely, notwithstanding an almost prohibitory duty.

The straw of the various grains was worth, it is said, above $1,500,000.

The wheat is threshed in the primitive manner of the ancient Egyptians, with horses to tread it out, on a floor of pounded earth.

Rice, sarsaparilla, and *vanilla*. — The rice product of Mexico amounted to above $1,200,000 in 1880; yet the extent to which it is cultivated is not great, owing to the unhealthiness of localities where it flourishes.

Two wild vines, both of which are indigenous to Mexico, the sarsaparilla and the vanilla, contribute to the enrichment of the natives of the hot country. The vanilla, with the rich, aromatic fruitage, and spicy blossoms, is found growing in the tropical forests of Vera Cruz and Tobasco. It is carefully cherished, requiring skill and acquaintance with its habits for successful results, and its fruit yields above half a million dollars annual returns.

Sugar cane. — Three varieties of cane are planted in the Republic, known as the Castilian, Havana, and Otaheite. The first is not so full of juice as the others, but is more abundant in saccharine matter; the mixture of the three produces the best results in the manufacture of the sugar. The *tierras calientes* are especially adapted for the cultivation of the cane, and the plantations and the amount of improved machinery are increasing yearly. The methods of culture, and the processes for crushing the cane, and crystallization of the juice, are the same as those followed in Cuba and Porto Rico. The plantations are of great area, some producing from 2,000,000 to 3,000,000 pounds of sugar annually. The largest are situated in the states of Morelos, Jalisco, Vera Cruz, Oaxaca, Puebla and Yucatan.

Sugar-cane was an importation of the Spaniards, the Mexican-Indians extracting sweets only from the native honey, from the agave, which juice they called *metl*, and from the saccharine pith of the maize. It was brought into Mexico from the Canary Islands, by way of the West Indies; for the Spaniards planted cane in San Domingo as far back as 1520.

As early as 1553, sugar was exported from Mexico, from the ports of Vera Cruz and Acapulco, into Spain and Peru. In the early part of this century, according to Humboldt, several million of pounds were annually exported at Vera Cruz. He also estimated the rich soil of the State of Vera Cruz as being capable of producing twice the product of cane per acre as that of Cuba; and Ward (another authority), pronounced the same state able to supply sugar to all Europe. Yet, in spite of these predictions, Mexico has never realized the hopes of her friends in this direction. Either the native Indian element has developed a liking for sweets that their early task-masters would not allow them previously to indulge, when Mexico exported sugar to other Spanish colonies; or the foreign element aids largely in its consumption; for sugar does not figure largely in the list of exports. Indeed, there is not enough produced for home-consumption. And it may be added that, as Mexico's population develops a taste for the luxuries of life, as it is constantly augmented by accessions from the United States and Europe, the demand for sugar will so increase that it will be imported to a considerable extent. Protective duties now serve to keep out American sugar (especially the refined grades), which sells in Mexico at high prices. Perhaps the radical reason for the inability of Mexico's sugar-plantations to keep pace with the demand is, that the area suitable for cane-cultivation is necessarily restricted. The plantations are not all of them situated in the unhealthy hot lands, as cane can be raised in the *tierra templada*, as high as four thousand feet, and where the only fevers are the relatively mild intermittents; in truth, the finest and most beautiful haciendas that the writer can call to mind, many of which he visited, are in a region very salubrious, though of course, hot. Those of Oaxaca, which are quite productive, are in a valley quite temperate in character, and near the healthful capital of the state. But the superficial configuration of the Mexican territory, notably rough and mountainous, forbids any extent of fertile valleys, in the rich mould of which alone the cane will grow to perfection. Mexico can, undoubtedly, raise a much greater quantity of sugar than she does now, when settled peace shall have given her planters an opportunity to rebuild mills destroyed by revolutionists, and to bring into cultivation thousands of acres which have been neglected from the same cause.

Another factor in successful cane-raising, which is all-important in Mexico, is water; and unless the present irrigation facilities can be extended in some remarkable manner, the sugar product will never reach a point to admit of exportation to other countries. The estimated yield for 1880, was 70,000,000 kilograms, valued at $8,716,000. Of the 2,019,823,614 pounds of sugar, imported into the United States in the three years ending June 30th, 1880, only 1,792,171 pounds came from Mexico, less than one-tenth of one per cent.[1]

Tobacco. — Indigenous to Mexico at the time the Spaniards first set foot upon its soil, was a plant which has since become famous throughout the world, tobacco, called *yetl* by the Aztecs, and used by them as a mild narcotic. We have only to turn to the history of that country to find that the lords of Montezuma's court, and even the great chieftain himself, used it after their repasts, daintily smoking it through amber tubes, and finding it especially grateful for the midday *siesta*. Mexico may never, perhaps, take rank with Cuba as a tobacco-producing country, but within her borders, especially on the confines of the *tierra caliente* of the east coast, there is a soil particularly adapted to the growth of the plant, and an atmosphere and temperature favorable for ripening and curing it. The tobacco of Vera Cruz is rapidly winning its way to favor, and when sufficient care shall have been exercised in the manufacture of Mexican cigars, they will, in all probability, compete successfully with the Havanas. The region about Cordova has long been celebrated for its tobacco, which has yielded a large revenue to viceroys and other rulers of Mexico for two or three centuries. The production of 1880 is given as 7,504,990 kilograms, having a value in Mexico of $2,000,000.

---

[1] See "Commerce between the United States and Mexico," Washington, 1884.

MINERAL REGIONS OF MEXICO.

"Mexico," says Lyell, "originally consisted of granitic ranges, with intervening valleys, subsequently filled up to the level of the plateaus by subterranean eruptions, as igneous rocks of every geologic epoch to a large extent form the superstructure of the central plateau. The most elevated regions are composed, especially the high ranges, of plutonic and volcanic rocks, although a great portion of the plateau is metamorphic, and contains the greatest variety of ores." Says another authority: "A line drawn from the capital to Guanajuato, and thence northward to the southwestern point of Chihuahua, and southward to Oaxaca, thus cutting the main axis of upheaval at an angle of 45°, will intersect probably the richest known argentiferous region in the whole world!"

In a general way it may be said that a metalliferous vein runs through the entire cordillera of Mexico, extending from the mines of the Sierra Madre in Sonora, — in the far northwest, — to the gold-deposits of Oaxaca, in the extreme south. The mineral districts most distinguished for their productions of silver and gold are those of Guanajuato, Zacatecas, Fresnillo, Real del Monte, Pachuca, Catorce, Tasco, and Oaxaca.

As the relative importance of mines is largely due to their proximity to great centres of population, the mines of Pachuca, — including those of Real del Monte, Chico, Capula, Santa Rosa, etc., — should first claim attention, being distant from the capital less than seventy miles. This group, in the State of Hidalgo, covers an area of twenty-five kilometres from north to south, and thirty-three from east to west. A second cluster is that of the district of Tasco, and those of Zacualpan, Sultepec, Angangeo, Tlalpujahua, and Zimapan. These groups, with those of Oaxaca, describe a circuit round about the City of Mexico, though open towards the east with a radius of about two hundred kilometres.

The districts of Guanajuato and Zacatecas form two groups, important for their numerous and industrious population. An offshoot from the main cordillera is the district of Catorce, north of San Luis Potosi. The states of Sonora, Oaxaca, Michoacan, Chihuahua, and Guerrero, abound not only in the precious metals, but in copper, iron, lead, zinc, etc. The most notable of these are the hills of iron in Durango and Oaxaca, and the copper found in Michoacan, and Chihuahua. Humboldt divided the Mexican mines into eight groups: the first, and most considerable, includes the almost contiguous districts of Guanajuato, San Luis Potosi, Catorce, Fresnillo, and Sombrerete; those to the west of Durango and Sinaloa form the second; the third group comprehends the mines of Chihuahua, and is the most northern; northwest of Mexico City lies the Real del Monte or Pachuca; those of Zimapan or el Doctor, the fifth; Bolanos, in Guadelajara, is the central point of the sixth; Tasco, of the seventh, and the mines of Oaxaca the eighth.

That part of the Mexican mountains containing the greatest quantity of silver lies between the parallels of 21° and 24° 30′ north latitude.

"It is remarkable," says Humboldt, (then, of course, being ignorant of the vast deposits of Nevada and Arizona), "that the metallic wealth of Mexico and Peru should be placed at an almost equal distance, in either hemisphere, from the equator."

HISTORY OF MEXICAN MINES.

"The mountains of Anahuac," wrote the celebrated historian Clavigero, a century ago, "abound in ores of every kind of metal. The Mexicans found gold in the countries of the Cohuixcas, the Miztecs, the Zapotecs and several others. They gathered it chiefly in grains amongst the sands of the rivers, and the above mentioned people paid a certain quantity in tribute to the crown of Mexico. Silver was dug out of the mines of Tlachco and Tzompanco. Of copper they had two sorts,—one hard, which they used instead of iron to make axes, mattocks, and other instruments of war and agriculture; the other flexible for the making of basins and other vessels. This metal abounded formerly in the provinces of Zacatollan and the Cohuixchas; at present it is found in the kingdom of Michoacan.

They dug tin from the mines of Tlachco, and lead from the mines of Izmiquilpan, a place in the country of the Otomies. Of tin they made money, and they sold lead in the market; there were likewise mines of iron in Tlascala, in Tlachco (Tlasco) and other places; but they either did not find out these mines,—or, at least did not know how to benefit themselves by the discovery. Mines of quicksilver they had in Chilapan, and in many places mines of sulphur, alum, vitriol, cinnabar, ochre, and a white earth strongly resembling white lead. Of amber and asphaltum, there was, and still is, a great abundance on both coasts, and they were both paid in tribute to the king of Mexico from many places of the empire. With respect to precious stones, there were, and still are, diamonds, though few in number; amethysts, cats-eyes, turquoises, cornelians, and some green stones, resembling emeralds (*Chalchinitls*); and of all these stones the Miztecs, Zapotecs, and Cohuixcas, in whose mountains they were found, paid a tribute to the king. The mountains which lie on the coast of the Gulf of Mexico, between the port of Vera Cruz and the river Coatzacoalco, namely, those of Chinantla, furnished them with crystal. There were quarries of jasper, and marble of different colors, in the mountains of Calpolalpan, to the east of Mexico, in the *Monte de las Cruces*, and in the Zapotec country; of alabaster (Mexican onyx) in Tecalco (now Tecale) State of Puebla, and in the country of the Miztecs; of *tezontli*, in the vale of Mexico itself, and in many other places of the empire. There are, besides, mountains of loadstone (magnetic iron), of the *Quitzalitztli*, or nephritic stone; the Mexicans formed various and curious figures; *Chimaltizatl*, which is a kind of talc, on calcination, gives a fine plaster, which the Mexicans used to whiten their paintings; the *Mezenitlatl* was the opal, very abundant. But no stone was more common with the Mexicans, than the *itztli*, or obsidian, of which they made mirrors, knives, etc."

That the ancient Toltecs and Aztecs obtained gold and silver, not only from the beds of mountain torrents and the auriferous sands of the coast streams, but from shafts and galleries sunk at great expense of time and toil, we have abundant proof. Like the native of Peru, they worked mines that dated their origin from a period so remote that no man knew when they were begun. The abundance of gold and silver vessels and bars of the precious metals at the time of the arrival of the Spaniards proves the above statement, aside from their own historic records. They possessed, besides gems, also cinnabar, lead, tin, and copper. The southern provinces paid tribute, not only in the peculiar products of their fields and forests, but in golden grains, as found in the rivers, and cast into bars, and wonderfully wrought ornaments.

Fortunately for the seeker after early statistics, we have an account of the ancient sources of wealth of the Aztecs in the letters of the conqueror himself; for Cortés wrote an explicit account of them to his sovereign. After getting Montezuma into his power, in the year 1520, he obtained from the Aztec ruler a list of all his mines. The account cannot be better rendered than in his own words: "When I discovered that Montezuma was fully devoted to your Highness, I requested him that, in order to enable me to render a complete account to your Majesty of the productions of the country, he would point out to me the mines from which gold was obtained, to which he consented with the greatest readiness. He immediately sent for several of his public servants, and assigned them to four provinces, two to each, in which he said the gold was obtained, and he asked me to allow some of the Spaniards to go with them that they might observe the manner in which gold was procured, and I accordingly deputed two Spaniards for the same number of his own men. One party of them went to a province called Cuzula, eighty leagues from the great city of Temixtitlan (Mexico), whose inhabitants are vassals of Montezuma, where they were shown three rivers, from all of which they brought me specimens of gold of a good quality, though procured with little trouble, and without any other instruments than those used by the Indians. . . . Another party of our envoys went to a province called Malinaltebeque, which is seventy leagues from the great city, but more towards the seacoast. They brought me specimens of gold from a great river that passes through it. The other party visited a region beyond this river, inhabited by a people speaking a different language from those of Culua (Mexico), and whose territory is situated on a lofty and rough mountainous range, with a population inured to war, who fight with spears of twenty-five to thirty palms' length; he is independent of Montezuma. . . . . He would not admit the subjects of Montezuma, but allowed the Spaniards to enter, and showed them seven or eight mines, from which they said gold was procured; and in their presence some of the Indians got out a quantity of the precious metal, of which specimens were brought to me. . . . . The other party of envoys visited a province called Tuchitebeque, on the same route, towards the sea, twelve leagues from the province of Malinaltebeque, where, I have already said, gold was found, and where they were shown two other streams, from which they obtained gold."

The first silver sent from the mines of New Spain was obtained from those of Tasco, discovered in the year 1522. These mines, with those of Pachuca, are considered the oldest in Mexico, some of them having been long worked by the Indians at the time of the arrival of the Spaniards. The amount of gold and silver obtained from Montezuma and sent to Spain is estimated at $7,000,000. This includes the household treasures of Axayacatl, his royal father, the accumulation, probably, of many years.

"The working of the mines of Zacatecas," says Humboldt, "followed closely after; one, the vein of San Barnabe, was begun in 1540, but twenty-eight years after the death of Montezuma. The principal vein of Guanajuato (*la Veta Madre*) was discovered somewhat later, in April, 1558. The dates of discovery of the most important Mexican veins, are as follows: Parral, in 1600; Cieneguilla, 1608; Guazapares, 1628; Urique, 1630; Batopilas, 1632; Cusihuiriachic, 1666; Chihuahuilla, 1671; Santa Eulalia, 1704; Topago, 1750; San Joaquin, 1774; Umapa, 1778; El Refugio, 1810; Jesus Maria, 1821; Palmares, 1824; Morelos, 1826;

Setentrian, 1829; Batougachic, 1839; Santo Domingo, 1867; Guadaloupe, 1869; Zapuri, 1873.

There were, by the calculation of Humboldt, at the opening of this century, five hundred places (*reales*, or *realitos*), celebrated for their mines, comprehending nearly five thousand mines (*minas*), or separate excavations. The principal *reales* were: — Guanaxuato, in the Intendency of the same name; Catorce, San Luis Potosi; Zacatecas, Zacatecas; Real del Monte, Mexico; Bolanos, Guadalaxara; Guarisamey, Durango; Sombrerete, Zacatecas; Tasco, Mexico; Batopilas, Chihuahua; Zimiapan, Mexico; Fresnillo, Zacatecas; Ramos, San Luis Potosi; Parral, Chihuahua.

With the increasing prosperity of the mines the *reales* were converted into pueblos or villages, giving an impulse to agriculture in the surrounding country, and to commerce, many of them finally becoming prosperous cities, which either drove away the Indians, or reduced them to submission and to a civilized life. Such is the history of the foundation of Guanajuato, whose real was established in 1554, obtained the title of town in 1619, and of city the eighth of September, 1741.

The natural mineral wealth of Guanajuato attracted attention from the very first. The first worked silver vein was that of San Bernabe, which afterwards belonged to the famous mine of La Luz. This vein, we are assured, was discovered by an *arriero* (muleteer), who travelled between Zacatecas and Mexico. Later, they worked Mellado and Rayas, and in sinking shafts in 1558, discovered the famous *Veta Madre*, — or Mother Vein, — which, since that epoch, has been attacked at various points, calling into existence the numerous mines of Valenciana, Tepeyac, Cata, Santa Anna, Fraustos, Santa Anita, and others, whose riches have attracted the attention of the old continent, even by the vast amount of its argentiferous products. The mines have suffered various vicissitudes; they have fallen away in production since the time when Humboldt published a statement of their almost fabulous yield. The mine of Guadalupe, known as the Cata, has been one of the richest and most famous of those in the district of Guanajuato. At the end of the eighteenth century it belonged to the heirs of the Marquis of San Clemente. Since the year 1758, it has been filled with water to such an extent that it could not be worked. If the mine could be effectually drained, it would also be possible to work the mine of San Lorenzo, an old and very rich one; and it is the general belief that when the *tiro principal*, — great main shaft, — shall be completed and these mines thoroughly drained, there will soon result such a bonanza as will revive the ancient splendors of Guanajuato.

"We may make," says a competent authority, "three periods in the history of Mexican silver mining: the Aztec period, which terminated at the arrival of the Spaniards, who inaugurated the second, which extended until Mexican independence, with continually increasing products. The Spaniards invented amalgamation by the *patio* process. Then came above twenty years of confusion, when little was done; but when the Republic had fairly got under way, and the country was, in some measure, open to foreigners, Europe, especially England, in hot haste to take advantage of the opportunity, sent over engineers and machinery and great sums of money, much of which was quite wasted, to the hopeless ruin of a great part of the adventurers. The improvements and machinery remained, however, but the mines passed into other hands. Of late years the companies have been doing well, and now export nearly as much silver as during the latter years of the Spanish Government."

The English minister, Ward, in writing of the mines of the table-land, said:—
. . "Fortunately there is no reason whatever to apprehend the approach of that scarcity of mineral productions with which many think Mexico is menaced. Hitherto, at least (1827), every step that has been taken in exploring the country, has led to fresh indications of wealth, which in the north appears to be really inexhaustible." (This was written twenty years before the discovery of gold in California, and when the territory comprising Arizona, Nevada, etc., was a howling wilderness.)

"Mining in Mexico has hitherto (true yet) been confined to a comparatively narrow circle; the immense mass of silver which the country has yielded since the conquest has proceeded from a few central spots; yet, if one examine these spots we shall find that three centuries of constant productiveness have not sufficed to exhaust the principal mines originally worked, while by far the largest proportion of the great veins remain unworked in each."

At Sombrerete, the vein of the Pavellon has been worked from the time of the conquest, though it was only in the year 1792 that it produced the famous bonanza. . . . . The mines of Santa Eulalia, in Chihuahua, continued to be equally productive during a period of eighty years, and were only abandoned at last in consequence of the incursions of the Indian tribes. The riches of Real del Monte can hardly be said to have diminished in a term of sixty years, although the difficulty of drainage caused the works there to be suspended. An account of the miners, on oath, in 1801, of the state of the lower levels, when abandoned, shows the richness of the vein to have been unimpaired.

TOTAL PRODUCT OF THE MEXICAN MINES.

A very clear estimate of the precious metals sent from the New to the Old World in the early years of its conquest is given by Humboldt, as follows: From 1492 to 1500, $15,000, gold of Cibao (Hayti), coast of Paria, etc. From 1500 to 1545, annual product $3,000,000: Mexican mines of Tasco, Zultepeque, Pachuca; Peruvian mines of Caxamarca and Cuzco, and the spoils of Tenochtitlan, Choco and Antioquia. From 1545 to 1600, $11,000,000: Zacatecas, Guanajuato, Cerro del Potosi, Peru, etc. From 1600 to 1700, $16,000,000: mines of Potosi getting exhausted, but new ones discovered. From 1700 to 1750, $22,500,000 alluvial deposits of Brazil, Mexican mines of La Biscaina, Sombrerete, and Batopilas. From 1750 to 1800, $35,500,000; last period of splendor of Tasco mine; the Valenciana wrought. The same great authority estimates the total gold and silver sent from America to Europe,—between years 1492 and 1803,—three centuries,—at £1,166,775,322; say in round numbers, $8,250,000,000.

Taking as a basis the estimates of the great Humboldt, the annual average of the Mexican mines between 1690 and 1803 was $12,000,000; and the total product up to 1884 will foot up nearly $4,000,000,000, as follows:—

Between 1521 — 1803 (inclusive)	. . . . .	$2,027,952,000
" 1804 — 1847 "	. . . . .	768,188,420
" 1848 — 1875 "	. . . . .	702,000,000
Product for 1876 (Cubas)	. . . . .	20,000,000
" " 1877 -'78 - '79 (estimated)	. . .	75,000,000
" " 1880 (Busto: *Estadistica*)	. . . .	29,713,355
" " 1881 — 1884 (inclusive: estimated)	. .	100,000,000
		$3,722,853,775

These estimates are, of course, more or less imperfect. No one can doubt the integrity of the great author of Cosmos, who diligently searched the mining records of Mexico, to which he had free access. "But," says an English authority, "during the civil war (which occurred ten years later, and lasted nearly twelve years), the archives, not only of the college of mines (to which Humboldt had access, and by which the produce of each separate district might have been ascertained), but of almost all the mining deputations, were destroyed Even the registers of the sums paid to the *Cajas Provinciales*,—provincial treasuries,—as the 'king's fifth,' have disappeared."

Our authorities, then, from which the foregoing deductions are made are: first, Humboldt (1803), Ward (1827), Brantz Mayor (about 1842), Cubas (1876), Busto, — *Estadistica de la Republica Mexicana* (1880), various Mexican writers scattered throughout the sixty years known as the Revolutionary period, and the *anuarios* (annuals) up to 1884. Ward, the British Minister to Mexico in 1827, thought that Humboldt under-estimated the product of the Mexican mines. He further alludes to the fact that from the mines, throughout the long period when Mexico was in the throes of civil strife, the lower classes drew their entire subsistence, by extracting ore from the upper levels of mines abandoned by their wealthy owners, and thus completing the ruin water had commenced by removing pillars left for support, etc. It is not the author's desire to make out a case either for or against the Republic of Mexico, but it is his wish to clearly present an accurate statement of its resources. It is his opinion that, considering the vast amount that conjecturally has paid no duties; has been smuggled out of the country, and extracted by the thousands of *buscones*, or illegitimate miners, of which no record has been kept, the mines of Mexico have yielded a total product of not less than $4,000,000,000.

In 1876, an American statistician,[1] basing his estimates upon those of Humboldt, and the various official reports of Great Britain and the United States, sums up the total products of gold and silver of the territory formerly known as New Spain, the most valuable portion of which the United States acquired from Mexico, in 1848, as follows:—

Mexico, 1521 — 1804	$2,027,052,000
" 1804 — 1848	768,188,420
" 1848 — 1876	702,000,000
California, 1848 — 1876	1,064,628,502
Nevada, 1848 — 1876	293,233,910
Arizona, 1848 — 1876	7,962,000
New Mexico, 1848 — 1876	6,075,000
Utah, 1848 — 1876	17,472,773
Total of New Spain 1521 — 1876	$4,887,512,605

He further compares the gold and silver product of the world, for about the same period, with that of New Spain, by which it appears that the latter restricted territory produced *thirty-seven per cent* of the whole, during three centuries:— New Spain, $4,858,512,605; the World, $13,111,825,889.

---

[1] Alex. D. Anderson, in The Silver Country; or, The Great Southwest. New York: 1877.

By a series of comparisons he shows that the greater portion of the world's silver product, of later years, has been obtained from New Spain:—From 1521 to 1804, it yielded 43 per cent of the silver product of the whole world; from 1804 to 1848, 56 per cent; from 1848 to 1868, 50 per cent; and during the year 1875, 75 per cent of the silver product of the whole world.

"The territory acquired by the United States from Mexico, produced," he says, "between 1848—1876 *seven-eighths* the total amount of silver and gold of the country, viz:—

Total product of United States	$1,574,045,802
" " " territory acquired from Mexico	1,389,372,185
" " " other States, only	$184,673,617."

RESUMÉ OF MINES AND MINING FOR THE YEAR 1880.

Mineral districts		324
Placers		23
Mines in working	1,247	
" "Denounced"	447	
		1,694
" of silver and gold	332	
" silver	807	
" copper	156	
" lead	143	
" cinnabar	94	
		1,694
Annual production in *cargas* (300 lbs. each)		2,567,306
" " in kilograms of pure metal		843,058,000
Value of total production of the mines		$29,713,355
Number of men employed		102,240
Salaries and wages paid		$8,021,000
Kilograms of pure silver reduced (*patio*)	360,284,317	
" " " " (*tonel*)	24,503,843	
" " " " (lixiviation)	16,077,771	
" " " " (*fuego*)	142,224,667	
		543,120,598
Number of mints in the Republic		11
Gold coined during year 1879	$622,524.00	
Silver " " " "	21,405,331.00	
Copper " " " "	16,300.00	
		$22,084,155.20
Kilograms of pure gold (961,131) value of		$618,514.58
" " silver (543,120,598) value of		$21,240,904.59
" " metal (544,081,720) value of		$21,859,419.17
Difference in kilograms between production and coinage,		299,938
" in value " " and "		$7,629,199.80

GOLD.

"Rivers become less auriferous," wrote Humboldt, "in proportion as, in the course of ages, their flow becomes less rapid. A horde of savages who settle in a valley where man has never before penetrated, find grains of gold, accumulated there for thousands of years; while in our day, the most careful washings hardly produce a few particles."

In corroboration of this we may cite the golden streams of Hayti and San Domingo which were so productive in the few years succeeding the discovery of the West Indies, but which now contain nothing of value. Mexican gold, the same great authority states, is for the most part extracted from alluvial ground, by means of washing. These grounds are common in the province of Sonora; a great deal of gold has been collected among the sands of the valley of the Rio Hiaqui (Yaqui). Farther to the north in Pimeria Alta, under the thirty-first degree of latitude, lumps of native gold, *pepitas*, have been found of the weight of from five to six pounds. In these desert regions, the incursions of the Indians, the excessive price of provisions, and the want of the necessary water for working, are all great obstacles to the extraction of gold.

Another part of the Mexican gold is extracted from the veins which traverse the primitive mountains, which are most frequent in Oaxaca (State), either in gneiss or micaceous slate, which last rock is particularly rich in gold. These veins, of which the *gangue* is milk quartz, are more than half a metre in thickness, but their richness is very unequal, as they are frequently "strangled," and the extraction of gold in the mines of Oaxaca is in general by no means considerable. Gold is to be found, either pure or mixed with silver ore, and there is scarcely a single silver mine which does not also contain gold. Native gold is frequently found crystallized in octahedrons, or as laminae, or in a reticulated form, in the silver ores of the mines of Villalpando and Rayas, near Guanajuato; Guarisamay, west of Durango; and Mezquitl, in Guadalajara, which last yields the purest metal.

Among the ancient Aztecs, the Spaniards found a great quantity of ornaments and works in gold, such as a golden disk, as large as a cart wheel, etc. Of presents to royalty, from the *conquistadores* of the New World, probably few have surpassed, in novelty of design, and intrinsic value, that golden culverin sent to the king of Spain by Cortés, in 1523. It was a superbly executed work, and valued at 20,000 ducats. In the great market of ancient Mexico, gold dust was sold in tubes, or quills of aquatic birds, made transparent, so that the size of the golden grains could be seen.

Although long celebrated as the Land of Gold, Mexico has not actually shown any great extent of territory that may be called auriferous. A glittering thread of gold runs, indeed, the entire length of the Sierra Madre, but it is only at rare intervals that it has been taken up and pursued with profit. Placer gold has been discovered in the north, but it is mainly in the south, in Oaxaca, that the ore has of late years been mined. The following list identifies auriferous localities:

NATIVE GOLD.—State of Guerrero, mineral de Tepantitlan; State of Mexico, mineral del Oro; State of Oaxaca, mineral de San Antonio.

AURIFEROUS PLACERS.—Several districts in the states of Chihuahua, Sonora, and Ixtapa in Mexico.

GOLD COMBINED WITH OTHER METALS.—State of Chihuahua: Guadalupe y

GOLD AND SILVER DISTRICTS.

Calvo, Guadalupe de los Reyes, Parral; State of Durango: Avino, Basis, Canelas, Comercio, Coneho, Cuencame, Duraznito, El Oro, Gavilanes, Guanacevi, Huahuapan, Inde, Mapimi, Penon Blanco, Picotercot, San Dimas, San Juan de Guadalupe, San Bruno, San Rafael, Santa Rosa, Santiago, Topia, Ventanas; State of Guerrero: mineral de Tasco; State of Guanajuato: The greater part of the mines of silver of the district of Guanajuato contain traces of gold, principally those of Rayas, Monte de San Nicolas, Sirena and el Nayal; State of Hidalgo, Pachuca, Zimapan; State of Jalisco, mineral de Etzatlan; State of Mexico: mineral districts, El Oro, Ixtlahuaca, Sultepec, Temascaltepec; State of Michoacan: minerals of Anganguco and Tlalpujahua; State of Oaxaca, minerals of Ixtlan and Penoles; State of Puebla, mineral de Tetela, del Oro; State of Queretaro, mineral del Doctor; State of San Luis Potosi, mineral of San Pedro; State of Sinaloa: Birimosa, Cajon, Cosala, Fresnos, Limon, San Javier, Tule; State of Sonora: Promontorios, Minas Nuevas; State of Zacatecas, Carcamo. Cedros, Chalchihuites, Fresnillo, Mazapil, Noria, Pico de Freire, Pinos, Zacatecas.

SILVER.

Mexico's greatest mineral wealth, undoubtedly, lies in its vast deposits of silver, as compared with which its treasure of gold is almost insignificant. In our general remarks upon mining, we have described the ancient and modern silver mines, and have related the history of their discovery. It only remains, now, to indicate the districts in which silver is the principal product. For further particulars, the reader is referred to the detailed description of the resources of the states.

NATIVE SILVER, says Humboldt, which is much less abundant in America than is generally supposed, has been found in considerable masses, sometimes weighing more than two hundred kilograms, in the mines of Batopilas. From time to time, he adds, small branches, or cylindrical filaments, of native silver, are discovered in the celebrated vein of Guanajuato; but these masses have never been so considerable as those which were formerly drawn from the mines of Encino, near Pachuca, and Tasco, where native silver is sometimes contained in foliated gypsum. It is now found in certain districts of Batopilas, State of Chihuahua, Guanajuato, Pachuca and Zacatecas; and argentiferous and platiniferous deposits in the district of Jacala, State of Hidalgo, known as Santa Maria de Alamos.

PRINCIPAL SILVER DISTRICTS.—Chihuahua: Batopilas, Batuchique, Candamena, Cusihuiriachi, Guadalupe y Calvo, Guadalupe de los Reyes, Jesus Maria, Morelos, Parral, Santa Eulalia, Toquimbo, Urique, Uruachi, Valle, Zapori.

Durango: Arzati, Avino, Bajada, Basis, Canelas, Coneto, Comercio, Cuencame, Durangal, Duraznito, El Oro, Fresnos, Gavilanes, Guanacevi, Huahuapan, Inde, Mapimi, Metatitos, Mezquital, Parrilla, Penon Blanco, Picoeterco, Pueblo Nuevo, Rodeo, San Dimas, San Juan de Guadalupe, San Lucas, Santiago, Sianori, Tamazula, Tejame, Topia, Ventanas.

Guanajuato: El Nayal, El Nopal, Gilmonene, Jesus Maria, La Joya, Mejiamora, Monte de San Nicolas, Rayas, San Pedro, Santa Lucia, Sirena, Socavon de San Cayetano, Valenciana.

Guerrero: Colorin, Socavon, Tasco, Zarza Nueva.

Hidalgo: Pachuca, Zimapan.

Jalisco: Bramador, Cuale, Etzatlan, Hoztotipaquillo, Huachinango, Ixtlan, La Bautista, La Yesca, San Sebastian, Santo Tomas.

Mexico · Chalchitepec, El Oro, Ixtlahuacan, Sultepec, Temascaltepec, Villa del Valle, Zacoalpan.

Michoacan: Agangueo, Tlalpujahua,

Morelos: San Juan de Dios.

Nueva-Leon: Mienas Viejas, in the district of Villaldama.

Oaxaca: Ixtlan, Penoles, Talea, Totoloapan.

Puebla: Tetela del Oro.

Queretaro: El Doctor.

San Luis Potosi: Bermalejo, Catorce, Charcas, Guadalcazar, Matehuale, San Pedro.

Sinaloa: Alisitos, Atotonilco, Bacubirito, Birimoa, Cajon, Calabazas, Cantarranas, Capula, Cosala, Chichi, Fresnos, Fuerte, Joya, Limon, Panuco, San Ignacio, San Javier, San Jose de Gracia, San Lorenzo, San Luis, Santa Cruz, Sarabia, Tigre, Tule, Yedras, Zapote.

Sonora: Aduana, Alamos, Baucari, La Barranca, La Trinidad, Los Bronces, Minas Nuevas, Soyopa, Tesopaco, Zuviate.

Zacatecas: Bolanos, Carcamo, Cedros, Chalchihuites, Fresnillo, Mazapil, Noria, Nieves, Sombrerete, San Juan de Guadalupe, Sierra Hermosa, Pinos, Rio Grande, Teul, Pico de Freire, Zacatecas.

The mineral districts given above are those from which was obtained the silver coined in the mints of the Republic during the fiscal year ending June 30, 1879, a total amount of $22,067,855

SULPHURET OF SILVER is found in Guanajuato, Pachuca, Zacatecas and in Zaculapan, State of Mexico. Ruby silver in Morelos, State of Chihuahua. Black silver in Chihuahua, Guanajuato and Zacatecas. Argentiferous galenite in the greater part of the mines of the Republic.

QUICKSILVER.

Cinnabar is found in the State of Durango: Pregones and Chiltepi; State of Guerrero: El Puesto, Jalisco; Guadalcazar, San Luis Potosi; El Doctor, Queretaro, and la Trinidad; in the cerro de Tippocanes, State of Zacatecas. Hepatic cinnabar in Guadalupe Atargea, State of Guanajuato. Guadalcazarite in Guadalcazar, State of San Luis Potosi. Onofrita in mine of San Onofre, State of Queretaro. Livingstonite in Huitzuco, State of Guerrero.

By referring to Humboldt, we find that New Spain in 1803 consumed an annual amount of 2,100,212 Troy pounds of mercury. "The court of Madrid, having reserved to itself the exclusive right of selling mercury, both Spanish and foreign, entered in 1784 into a contract with the Emperor of Austria. When the price of mercury has progressively lowered, the working of the mines has gone on increasing. In 1590 a quintal of mercury was sold in Mexico for 187 piastres; but in 1750 the court distributed it to the miners at 82 piastres; in 1777 a royal decree fixed the price of the mercury of Almaden at 41 piastres, 2 reales, and that of Germany at 63 piastres." From an argument by General Rosecrans, before Congress, in December, 1882, it appears, that, during thirty-three years, the quicksilver-mines of California have produced 1,310,095 flasks, or 100,222,267 pounds. California produces half the quicksilver of the world; that of the Old World, from the mines of Austria and Spain, being controlled by the Rothschilds, who, but for the mines of California and Mexico, would seriously retard all mining operations, to which this valued product is essential in the reduction of ores.

IRON.

Meteoric iron is found in the desert of San Carlos, State of Coahuila, and Jiquipilco, State of Mexico. Magnetic iron in "Encarnacion," State of Hidalgo, and in the State of Chihuahua. Red globular iron in Cerro del Mercado, in the State of Durango. Plumbago in the district of Zimapan, State of Hidalgo.

Further allusion to the great mass of iron ore known as *el Cerro del Mercado* will be found under the Mines of Durango. Meteoric masses have been discovered in various portions of Mexico. Says a writer on Mexico: "The 'Arabian Nights' story of the mountain which consisted of a single loadstone finds its literal fulfilment in Mexico. Not far from Huetamo, on the road to the Pacific, there is a conical hill, composed entirely of magnetic iron ore. The blacksmiths in the neighborhood, with no other apparatus than their common forges, make it directly into wrought-iron, which they use for all ordinary purposes."

COPPER, LEAD, SULPHUR, AND VARIOUS MINERALS.

Common pyrites are found in mine of La Mala Noche, Zacatecas. Radiated pyrites in mines of Guanajuato and Zacatecas. Lead in Galena and Zimapan, State of Hidalgo; and Asientos, State of Aguascalientes. Carbonate of lead in mine of San Nicola and Maconi, State of Queretaro; mine Negra in Jacala and Zimapan, State of Hidalgo. Sulphite of copper in Tepezala, State of Aguascalientes. Yellow copper in Santa Clara, State of Michoacan; Santa Rosalia, Chihuahua, and Agua Blanca, Jalisco. Native bismuth, in mine of Orito and in Ojo Caliente, State of Zacatecas. Bismuth silenide in mine of Santa Rosa, State of Guanajuato. Carbonate of bismuth in the Cerros del Desierto, State of San Luis Potosi. Ochre of bismuth in Vizarron, State of Queretaro. Zinc in mines of Tasco, State of Guerrero. Native sulphur in volcano of Popocatepetl; Orizaba, State of Vera Cruz, and Taximaroa, Michoacan.

Regarding the ancient use of copper, Humboldt wrote: "Of all the metals, copper was that which was most commonly employed in the mechanical arts: it supplied the place of iron and steel to a certain extent; and the arms of the Aztecs, axes, chisels, and all their tools, were made of the copper which they extracted from the mountains of Zacotollan and Cohuixco. Several men of great learning, but unacquainted with chemical knowledge, have maintained that the Mexicans and Peruvians possessed a particular secret for tempering copper, and converting it into steel. There is no doubt that the axes, and other Mexican tools, were almost as sharp as steel instruments; but it was by the admixture of *tin*, and not by any tempering, that they acquired this extreme hardness. . . . In several provinces (of Anahuac), pieces of copper to which the form of a T was given, were used as currency. Cortés relates, that having undertaken to found cannons in Mexico, and having despatched emissaries for the discovery of mines of tin and copper, he learned, that, in the environs of Tasco, the natives employed in exchange pieces of melted tin, which were as thin as the smallest coins of Spain." See also the author's text and cuts of ancient copper utensils, in "Travels in Mexico," p. 544.

PRECIOUS STONES, OPALS, ETC.

Rubies are found in the State of Durango. Diamonds in the State of Guerrero and Tonalixco, in the direction of the Sierra de Zongolica. Topazes in the Sierra de Canoas, in the State of San Luis Potosi. Emeralds in Tejupitco, State of Mexico. Garnets in Xalostro, State of Morelos, and in the State of Chihuahua. Fine opals in Esperanza and Amealco, State of Queretaro, and in Real del Monte, State of Hidalgo. Common opals in Zimapan, State of Hidalgo. Stilbite in States of Chihuahua and Guanajuato. Quartzes, agates, carnelians, etc., in Real del Monte, State of Hidalgo, and in the mine of San Rafael, State of San Luis Potosi. Various silicates in Bustamancia and Pachuca, State of Hidalgo. Xonatlacias in Xonotla, State of Puebla.

The richest opaliferous district is in Queretaro, in the environs of the hacienda of Esperanza, ten leagues (twenty-five miles) north-west of San Juan del Rio. This hacienda is surrounded by opal-bearing rocks; even the buildings pertaining to it being erected upon them. The opals of Esperanza were discovered in 1855 by a servant of the place, but were not worked until 1870, when the first mine was opened one league north-east of the hacienda, and called Santa Maria del Iris. Others followed, and now there are ten veins exposed. The rock in which the opals are found is a siliceous porphyry, the banks, or ridges, having a general direction from south-east to north-west, which may be plainly noted in the hill of *Ceja de Leon* — the Lion's Eyebrow. The mine called the Simpatica is the most noted for its great variety of opals, inasmuch as it is called a magazine of all known varieties. In the same morning one can obtain precious opals, *arlequines; fire-opals, — girasols de fuegos,* — semi-opals, etc.

The precious opals are found both opaque and transparent, and presenting an infinite play of color, from ruby and metallic lustre, to violet blue, which is considered as a rare and desirable color. The *arlequines* reflect a diversity of colors. The *girasols* display emerald tints upon a basic color of fiery red.

In the neighboring hills are the mines of El Rosario, El Iris, La Peineta, and Providencia. As the opals are encountered disseminated throughout the matrix of porphyry, without any apparent system, their mining consists merely in sinking various wells, or small shafts, on the most likely spots, making use of augers, — *barrenos,* — on account of the hardness of the rock containing the stones. When one of these shafts attains to a sufficient depth, it presents a really marvellous spectacle; the rock glistening with a thousand rays of colored light. The color of the matrix varies from a grayish red to a reddish white, and the difference in color indicates the class of opal it contains. In the first are found the *girasols*, or fire-opals, though mixed with others, similar; but in the white porphyries, as in those of the Cerro de Peineta, are found in profusion cloudy opals as beautiful as those of Hungary and Guatemala.[1]

MARBLE. — Sierra de Puebla; las Aguas and Vizarron, State of Queretaro; and in the States of Guerrero, Guanajuato, Michoacan, Nuevo-Leon, etc.

MEXICAN ONYX. — State of Puebla.

GYPSUM. — In Tamazula; State of Jalisco.

GRANITE. — State of Oaxaca; Ameca, State of Jalisco; Tamascaltepec, State of Mexico; and on the coast of Acapulco, State of Guerrero.

---

[1] *Estadistica de la Republica.*

OBSIDIAN. — The most important article obtained from the earth, to the Aztec, was obsidian, a volcanic glass, called by them *Itztli*, a knife, or shining stone. Ancient mines of it are found to-day in many localities, particularly in the Cerro de las Navajas, near Pachuca, about which are scattered, it is said, hundreds of tons of fragments. Everywhere, over plain and valley, may be encountered knives, arrow and spear points, of obsidian, showing how numerous were the uses to which it was put during the time of the early people of Mexico.

PORPHYRY. — Chihuahua: Hidalgo, Jalisco, Puebla, Queretaro, and Zacatecas.

POTTER'S CLAY. — In Guanajuato; and Leon of the same State.

SALT DISTRICTS. — Lower California, Colima, Jalisco, Michoacan; San Luis, Potosi; Tequesquites, Tamaulipas; Valley of Mexico; Yucatan and Zacoalco.

TEQUESQUITE. — The surface exposed by the subsidence of Lake Tezcoco is sterile, treeless, almost herbless, but a few inches above that of the lake itself. Only a few plants appear upon it, belonging to the genera of *Gratiola*, *Atriplex*, etc.; such, in short, as thrive in a soil highly impregnated with saline substances.

"The landscape," says a very intelligent writer, "is that of a dreary desert, in places resembling the African Sahara; but in other places more like a northern moorland, with a hoar-frost, or a slight sprinkling of snow upon the ground; for here the *tequesquite* appears, coating the surface, sometimes of a snow-white color, sometimes with a yellowish tinge. It is the *natron*, a mixture of carbonate and sulphate of soda. The poor people dwelling around the lake collect and bring it to market; and it is employed in various ways, — for washing, for the fabrication of soap, and also in the cooking of one of the most common of Mexican dishes, the *frijoles*. They also manufacture a coarse kind of salt out of the earth thus impregnated, by a rough process known to them in the days of Montezuma. It seems to ooze out of the earth, forming an efflorescence on the surface, sometimes to the extent of a uniform stratum of an inch or so in thickness."

There is a very extensive deposit of this mineral salt in the State of Zacatecas, from which the miners of that section draw large quantities for use in smelting. This saline incrustation is formed on the surface of a shallow lake, which in a good year was estimated to yield 30,000 *fanegas*, or 360,000 *arrobas* (twenty-five pounds) yearly, and which was formerly worth one dollar the mule-load. The deposition depends upon the season, being best and thickest with an average rainfall. The only preparation it needs is to be gathered into conical, earth-covered hillocks, whence it is taken away by the purchasers.

COPPERAS. — In Tepeji, State of Mexico; Barranca de Toliman, in Hidalgo; Taretan and Huetamo, State of Michoacan.

COALS, AND MINERAL OILS. — Anthracite: In Tequisquiapan, State of Queretaro, and Tecomatlan, Puebla.

PIT COAL. — In Tecomatlan, State of Puebla.

PETROLEUM. — Puerto Angel, State of Oaxaca.

NAPHTHA. — In Guadalupe, Hidalgo, federal district.

STONE COAL. — In Chamacuero, State of Guanajuato.

For further details, see Resources of the various States, Industries, etc.

MINING AND MILLING.

1st, Can ore-reducing be profitably carried on in this Republic so as to obtain through it an *income?* If so, to what extent?

2d, Which is the part of the country most suitable for reducing silver and gold ores?

3d, Which of the known mining districts or zones offers for the future the best mining prospects, or best probabilities to the industry of reducing ores?

In answer to these questions, Señor M'guel Rul, a leading mining engineer of Guanajuato, replies in substance through the columns of "The Two Republics" (an American paper published in Mexico), as follows: —

(1) "The income will be variable, — in one year, perhaps, enormous, but in another small. It is advisable to erect reduction-works, especially for any one mine, but, where transportation is low, better to make one establishment suffice for a large group of mines.

"My answer is therefore divided in two parts: Firstly, the business of reducing ores does not offer probabilities enough of yielding a lasting or perpetual *income*, as is the case, for instance, with a farm or a house; but, secondly, said business, like all others not consisting only in landed property, may render in good epochs large profits, with which the capital laid out may be reimbursed."

(2) Guanajuato he considers the place at which reduction is best carried on.

(3) "As regards the third question, I believe, that, in our times, the most suitable places of all the ones actually worked, to establish such a kind of business, should be the environs of Pachuca and Mazapil (where I am not interested at all), those of Salvatierra (which would favor my Guanajuato business), and, towards the south, some places well fitted to reduce ores from the growing mining districts of Guerrero, Morelos, and Oaxaca. With respect to future centres, of mining districts scarcely worked, Chihuahua, Sonora, and Durango may be at once pointed out as the most preferable ones."

Señor Rul's description of the method of treating silver ores most used in Mexico is so valuable, that we herewith reproduce it. The "Patio System" originated in Mexico, and its use is peculiar to the country.

Granceo (crushing). — The first operation to which ores are submitted in order to reduce them consists in their being ground into small lumps in mills, called *Chilenos* (Chilians), substantially consisting of a large vertical iron or stone wheel pierced at its centre by a horizontal shaft, to which mules are attached to furnish motive-power. The ground upon which the wheel operates is a circle 0^m 49 wide, formed by iron pieces of the same material and thickness as the wheel-tire. Between this circle and the vertical shaft there is a sieve, in the shape of a truncate cone, into which lumps are shovelled, falling afterwards into a reservoir placed underneath the mill.

The crushed ores are taken to the hoppers, and thence to the grinding mills, or *arrastres*, where they are to be ground, or reduced to a very fine mud, — an operation upon which depends the quantity of silver and gold obtained. The locality where the *arrastres* are situated is called the *Galera*.

The *arrastre* is a circle 3^m 50 diameter, constructed with flags inserted into the ground, the interstices between them filled up with pebble, and then with fine sand

THE PATIO PROCESS.

and water. At the centre a large and thicker stone is placed, called *cepo* (stock), intended to receive a vertical post, called *peon*, which is turned by means of a pole, to which two mules are set to move the apparatus, dragging a large stone, hung by means of chains to each one of the cross-arms. These stones are called *voladoras* (runners). Their length is a little shorter than the radius of the *arrastre*. They are cut in four-face prisms, and weigh about nine hundred weight, and are, as well as those forming the bottom of the *arrastre*, a hard quartzose porphyry.

In constant operation, the runners last about two months, and the bottom stones, about sixteen months. The quantity of ore ground in one *arrastre* of the given dimensions, *de marca* (standard), varies from eight to twelve hundred weight. During the twenty-four hours required to grind said quantity of ore, twenty or twenty-six hundred weight of water is required.

The quantity of water put into an *arrastre*, and the manner of feeding it, have a great influence on the success of the grinding as well as on the amount of gold to be found in the sediment; and much depends upon the *capitan de galera*, or foreman.

When the ore is reduced to fine mud, after twenty-four hours' work, — that is to say, when at the bottom of the *arrastre* no sand is found, — the *arrastre* is discharged, provided the mud be not too curdy, which is shown by the hand emerging from it as if it were japanned. Such being the case, more water is to be added, and the mud to be tried again, after having worked it a little while.

When the sand is perfectly fine, the upper part of the contents of the *arrastre* is taken out, and new ore put into it to complete its load.

To discharge the *arrastre*, the mud is taken from it to large reservoirs, called *lameros*, where the mud worked every day is put together until having the necessary quantity to form a cake. The *arrastres* must not be totally emptied, because, however perfect the grinding may be, a certain portion of badly ground ore always remains at the bottom, besides running the risk of throwing into the reservoir a part of the amalgam which always exists at the bottom of the *arrastre*.

Extraction of Gold. — On commencing the grinding in an *arrastre*, either by having provided it with a new bottom, or by its having been scraped, the interstices between the bottom flags are filled up with fine sand; then, in order to level the *arrastre*, a small quantity of poor ore is ground. If the *arrastre* be not a new one, but only scraped, the fine sand may be dispensed with, as the grinding of poor ore serves the purpose. The *arrastre* being levelled, a quantity of quicksilver amalgamated with some other metal, as silver, copper, zinc, etc., is thrown to the bottom, — an operation which is called *empellar*, — taking care to evenly spread the amalgam on the bottom. The quantity of amalgam to be put into an *arrastre* depends upon the amount of gold contained in the ore, as well as upon the quantity of ore to be ground within the time elapsing between the scraping operations, according to custom or convenience.

In general, when eight hundred weight of ore are daily ground in an *arrastre*, twelve pounds of amalgam are employed, in which there are about nine and a half pounds of quicksilver. The quantity of amalgam put at the beginning of the operation is insufficient to gather all the gold and a portion of the silver contained in the ore, as in the course of the operation the amalgam loses its gathering property. Hence it is necessary to gradually add small quantities of quicksilver; to ascertain which, trials of the *arrastre* are made two or three times a week, or oftener if the ores be very rich, in order to know their condition. The trials are made as follows:

The *arrastre* is divided by the runners in four equal parts: when a trial is to be made, the runners are placed in a given position, which is to be changed at the moment of effecting the trial. One of the four compartments of the *arrastre* is emptied; and, when the bottom is exposed to view, small quantities of mud are taken from the interstices, forming with them balls, which are placed in an orderly manner in a box with compartments, numbered as the compartments of the *arrastre*, in order to avoid confusion.

The balls are washed; and from the appearance of the sediment the condition of the mud is ascertained. If the sediment appear compact, or divided in large pieces, it proves that the mud is well saturated with quicksilver, and the operation can go on; but should the mud be too much pulverized, almost powdered, then it is too dry, and wants more quicksilver, until it becomes as fluid as at the beginning of the operation. In the former case, the pressure of the mud with the finger forms a white and shining surface: in the latter instance, it forms a dark and opaque one. An accurate account of the quantity of quicksilver put into each *arrastre* is kept, so as to know at any moment the total amount employed in the *galera:* hence the approximate quantity of silver in all the *arrastres*. From ores without pure silver, ten or twelve per cent of the alloy contained in the whole grinding is gathered; but the best way to ascertain it is to assay the amalgam, taking small quantities from each trial in order to estimate the condition of the *galera*. Said assays show very accurately the amount of gold and silver contained in all the *arrastres*.

When the amalgam is considered rich enough, or when it is thought that its quantity at the bottom of the *arrastre* is too large (which would be detrimental to the grinding operation), the scraping operation is commenced. This consists in taking out the flags forming the bottom of the *arrastre*, extracting with hooks from the interstices all the earth which may contain amalgam. The operation ends, when, assaying the earth taken from the interstices, no amalgam is found in it. It would be no inconvenience, however, to leave a small quantity of amalgam in the earth, as it will be picked out when putting new bottom to the *arrastre*. The earth is washed, adding to it a suitable amount of quicksilver, and putting it into large trays, where the amalgam settles, containing about eighteen to twenty-two pounds of mixed silver for a hundred pounds of quicksilver used in the *galeras*.

Patio (*yard*).— The *patio* is a large yard paved with flags very well adjusted to each other, so as to prevent as much as possible the escaping of the quicksilver, and with declivity enough to allow the running of the rain-water without carrying the mud of the cakes which are to be placed over the flags. The cakes are formed with the ground ore which is to be worked upon. Whenever there is in the *lamero* (reservoir) mud enough to form a cake (about a hundred *montones*, though they are sometimes larger), the mud is thrown in the yard, taking care of daily taking out from the *lamero* any excess of water that may be there. The mud is received into another provisional reservoir, constructed over the yard in the space to be occupied by the cake, which reservoir is called *cajete;* and its size is such as to allow the mud to form a cake $0^m\ 25$ to $0^m\ 30$ thick. The cake is allowed to settle itself, being perforated now and then, to make the water on its surface gradually flow out. This operation, together with the spontaneous evaporation, prepares the cake for salting within four or six days. Before salting the mud, it must be assayed, taking from different points in the reservoir small quantities of mud by means of a wooden rod, which is pushed down to the bottom in order to have mud from the bottom, the centre, and the superficies of the cake. The mud thus collected is put together, well mixed up, and ready to effect the assay. The assay gives to the cake a richness lower than the one obtained when assaying the ground ore; which difference is caused both by the silver remaining in the *arrastre* and by the wear of the latter, which, increasing the bulk of the cake, abates its relative richness. The quantity of gold obtained in this assay will give an exact idea of the amount to be collected from the *arrastres*, consequently, of the degree of perfection attained in such an interesting operation. It is to be borne in mind that the assay of the cake, which serves as a basis to estimate the ore, as well as the results of the reduction, is made both by the miner who sells the ore and by the reducer who purchases it. Hence the results of two different assays show the true value of the ore, with a proper allowance for reduction, provided the operation be accurate. It is also to be borne in mind that it is untrue, as some misinformed foreign writers have asserted, that our assays show a richness thirty per cent lower than the right one; for, since the exportation of ores is allowed, many a quantity of them has been sold to Europe, the assays made there having given a result very similar to ours.

The quantity of salt to be put in a cake varies according to the richness of the ore, and it is impossible to state a constant proportion. We have only noticed that the fluctuation takes place in the same direction; that is to say, the richer the mud is, the larger the quantity of salt required; so that, for instance, when the quantity of silver in a *monton* is from four to six marks, 125 pounds of salt are required, which is equivalent to 3.90 per cent of the mud. If the richness be from six to ten marks, 150 pounds of salt will be added, say 4.68 per cent. On adding the salts to the cake, it must be evenly distributed over the surface in order that its action may be uniform on the whole mass.

Chlorure of sodium constitutes the active principle of salt, and is one of the agents indispensable for amalgamation. The common salt used in the reduction of ores contains other substances, such as chlorures of calcium and magnesium, sulphates of the same bases and of soda, carbonates of soda and lime, some earth, and other accidental substances. All those impurities being very variable, even in salts coming from the same mine, and having great influence upon the result and duration of ore-reduction, the salt must be assayed previous to being added to the cake in order to ascertain the quantity of chlorure of sodium it contains. Besides, it must be borne in mind that to employ poor salt, or to use an insufficient quantity of it, will prove very detrimental.

The cake being salted, with the above precautions, the first *repaso* is practised. *Repaso* is the name people give to the operation of stirring the mud mixed with the substances required for reducing ores, and is performed by mules, which are caused to continually walk over the cake during eight hours. Twenty-four mules generally are employed for a cake containing a hundred *montones* (about 147 net tons).

On the day following the salting of the cake; the *magistral* and quicksilver are added, an operation called *incorporo* (incorporation). Both the above substances are to be perfectly spread over the surface of the cake; which operation offers no difficulty at all, as the *magistral* is powdered, and the quicksilver is strained through a linen, pressed by hand, and takes the form of small balls, coming out like drops of rain. After having incorporated the cake, another stirring is immediately effected, repeating said operation every other day, from six in the morning to two in the afternoon. On the very day the stirring is made, the cake is overturned, so as to have the whole mass perfectly mixed up. This operation is made with shovels handled by men; its purpose being to cause the mud to be equally affected by the mules, the combination of the substances added, and the action of the sun.

The quantity of *magistral* used depends upon several circumstances, the main one being the amount of sulphate of copper it contains, as it is a well-known fact that said ingredient is a double sulphur of copper and iron, which by calcination assumes the condition of sulphate of the same metals, but mixed with variable quantities of metallic oxides. The kind of the ore to be reduced, and the atmospherical temperature, are also to be taken into consideration when stating the proportion. With regard to the first influence, it is obvious, that, the richer in sulphate of copper the *magistral* is, the smaller the quantity required. As a general rule, we may say that pure crystallized sulphate of copper is added at the rate of seven or eight pounds to a *monton* of ore having from five to eight marks of silver. As regards the second influence, — that is to say, the kind of ore to be reduced, — nothing but practice can ascertain it, and suggest the quantity of *magistral* to be used. Regarding the third influence, — viz., atmospherical temperature, — we can only state, that, under similar circumstances, less *magistral* is required in winter than in summer time. Quicksilver is in general put at the rate of four pounds to each mark of silver in the cake, as per the assay made before salting it, better still, as per the result of the assay made with the *granza*, deducting the metal which has remained in the *arrastres*. The quicksilver is put in smaller quantity than the one above mentioned; but, in the course of the reduction, small portions are gradually fed, when the assay hereafter alluded to shows that the amalgamation wants quicksilver.

After the cake has been incorporated and stirred, another experiment is made, called *tentadura*, in order to ascertain the effects the ingredients are producing. Said assay is practised every day, in the morning (also at noon, when the cake has been stirred), taking about half a pound of mud from different parts of the cake, — now from the superficies, now from the bottom, or from both, according to the purpose in view. The mud is dissolved in water contained in a dark-bottomed vessel, which is a small tray made of a gourd called *guaje*; then the mud is washed (taking care not to rub it either against the vessel or between the fingers) by a rotary movement, the water carrying away the earth and other useless parts; then, putting in clean water, the vessel is lightly shaken, so that the different components of the remaining sediment may take their respective places, according to their different densities, in order to be inspected; finally, a few drops of water are skilfully sprinkled with the fingers into the gourd, a little over the place occupied by the ore.

The characteristics of the ore are offal or refuse (called *lis de azogue*), limature, metallic sediment or fine powder, and a globule formed by the detached quicksilver. Offal, so called because it is the somewhat modified and greatly subdivided quicksilver, forms a white and tarnished stripe on the upper part of the ore, — a reason why it is also called *cabeza* (head), — and on being rubbed between the fingers forms small globules of quicksilver. Limature is a white and shining stripe, which on being rubbed with the thumb becomes a thin sheet of amalgam, called *pasilla*. The metallic sediment, also called body of the hard cake, is composed of the unreduced ore and some of the substances accompanying it.

The quicksilver globule at the bottom gives, when strongly compressed with the thumb, a certain amount of amalgam, which increases as the reduction advances.

Sometimes, when the reduction is near completion, the quicksilver does not form globules, but is diffused.

When the limature has the same color as the amalgam, and gives forth a small amount of silver; when the offal forms a narrow and opaque stripe; finally, when the globule is clear and shining, with little grains on its surface, and, strongly compressed with the finger, gives out an amalgam that makes in the gourd a white mark, — then it may be said that the reduction is going on the right way. If the offal be ash-colored, and the limature rather opaque and soft, thus showing its being overloaded with quicksilver; if, besides, the color of the globule be dark-gray, and the amalgam it contains, on being separated by pressure, leaves on the gourd a track very prominently white-colored, producing something like whitish smoke, — then it is said that the cake is *hot*. The degree of heating is estimated by the evidence of the aforesaid features. When the *lis* and limature are very scarce, and the latter too juicy (the globule being elongated and depressed, yellowish or blackish colored), and the amalgam rendered by it leaves no track on scraping the gourd, then it is said that the cake is *cold*.

In the trial made after the stirring following the incorporation, if the ore be not very rich, a narrow offal stripe and a small quantity of limature are all that appear at the top; hence, at the beginning of the reduction, if the ore be poor and rebellious, there is rather no other guidance than the quicksilver globules.

When the cake becomes hot during the first reduction days, the evil may be prevented by adding either a certain quantity of fresh mud from the reservoir, or some precipitate of copper; but, should the heating be noticed at the end of the operation, precipitate of copper, ashes, and salt should be put in.

The action of cold is overborne by throwing into the cake a small quantity of *magistral*, or sulphate of copper, in order to increase its strength.

When the reduction process goes on rightly, it may be noticed, that, on the twentieth day, the limature and metallic sediment the silver contains begin to decrease, while the globule abounds with amalgam; but those effects never appear before the thirtieth day when the ore is rebellious.

On the cake being ready, a rapid increase of quicksilver *lis* is noticed, which, rubbed with the finger, becomes quicksilver globules, the limature disappearing at the same time. But, although those features are very prominent, they may in many an instance be deceitful. Such is especially the case when quicksilver is in excess, and salt scarce, either for not having put at first the necessary quantity of it, or for it having been consumed or carried out by the rain-water. In order to avoid perplexity, the amalgam is assayed, thus ascertaining the amount of silver extracted; and this indication, in conjunction with the other characteristics previously found, gives the certainty that no larger amount of silver is to be extracted.

The above assays serve not only to show the yielding of the cake, but also the daily progress of the reduction process. It is a curious fact to be observed, that the results of the assays go on in a parallel line, so to say, with the indications of the amalgam, as hitherto explained; so that those two means complete each other.

Washing. — The reduction being finished at the yard, the cake is washed in order to separate the mass of crude metal from the muddy and terreous part. The washing-place is formed by three or four large wooden or stone and mortar vats communicating with each other through large square holes called *bilitrones*. The first and last of said vats have also outside openings, — the first one to receive the mud, and the last one to effect the discharging. Inside those vats is a four-arm churn-staff, which by its revolutions dissolves the mud, allowing the latter to remain at the surface of the water all the time necessary for the silver and quicksilver to settle themselves at the bottom. Before commencing to wash the cake, it must be softened by water in as large a quantity as to have the mud thoroughly fluid. Then the mud is carried through a large channel made on the very floor of the *arrastre*, dragging it along by means of a frame of laths pulled by a mule, until the mud is thrown into the first vat, called *cargadora*. When the filling operation is over, with the vats half-full with water, the churn is caused to rapidly revolve during half an hour,—an operation called *batir* (to beat); then the vats are filled up with water, the churn is slowly revolved (*asentar*, to settle) during an hour and a half, at least, in order to be sure of the operation; then the discharging follows. But a trial is made before, to see whether the settling has been perfectly made, introducing into the last vat but one a small vessel hermetically closed, which, when level with the vat-hole, is opened by means of a peculiar device, its contents being received into a gourd, there to be assayed. If the settling has been perfect, a stripe of quicksilver *lis* or offal appears, which on being rubbed does not form any globule, also some pyrites and terreous parts; but, should the stripe give forth any quicksilver globule, then the settling has been imperfect, and must be continued until the above-mentioned characteristics are obtained. Then the discharging begins, unstopping the last vat, called *piojo*, in order to have it emptied down to the opening level. Another assay is made, for security's sake, so that any defect noticed may be corrected at once.

The vats are filled up again, repeating all the aforesaid operations, until the whole of the cake is washed. Then comes the rinsing operation (*en juagar*), pouring fresh water into the vats, beating and settling again, so as to clean out all the mud.

As the quantity of mud put in each filling is proportional to the capacity of the vats, the washing takes more or less time. Vats 3m 35 diameter by 1m 67 deep, generally contain three or four *montones*. As each partial washing takes about two hours, to wash a cake of one hundred *montones* requires three or four days. When the respective situations of the yard and the washing-place do not allow the mud to be dragged as aforesaid, it is carried by men in large troughs.

Apurar (to purify).—This is the next operation, consisting in taking from the vats the settled metal, the larger part of which is found in the first vat, mixed up with *cabecilla*, that is to say, the ore, which, not being reduced to mud, appears like sand. This sand is put into large and deep troughs, which are kept over the water in a large basin, and undergo an oscillatory and revolving movement, so that the metal may settle at the bottom, adding to that end a quantity of quicksilver, which leads down the smaller particles.

As the metal so gotten contains, however, earth and other impurities, the cleansing operation (*limpia*) comes next, to have the metal completely purified. The mass of crude metal is taken to the *azogueria*, where it is thrown into a circular stone basin well covered with bitumen; more quicksilver is added to it, stirring it through, so that the impurities remain at the surface. If some hard grains be found, they are taken out and ground, incorporating them afterwards with the mass in the basin.

When the mass of crude metal is thoroughly cleaned, it must be dried, so as to have it in a mass condition. To obtain such an effect, the crude metal is thrown into a conical bag (*manga*), hung to a beam by means of strong chains. The upper part of said bag is made of hide, and of wool the lower one; so that the quicksilver may pass through its interstices. The very weight of the mass compressed into the bag causes the quicksilver to flow out; but, in order to quicken the operation, the bag is beaten with wooden mallets, until no quicksilver comes out.

The mass is then thrown into iron moulds, to form sectors of a cylinder, called *marquetas o bollos* (cakes or bars), afterward proceeding to separate by fire the quicksilver they may contain.

Roasting. — The roasting is done in an apparatus, called *capellina*, consisting of a circular cast-iron or copper vessel called *bacin*, and inserted into the floor, which is formed with fire-proof stones very well adjusted to each other and to the *bacin*. The superficies formed by those stones, which is called *planta*, has also a circular shape; the stones being cut in such a manner as to leave around the *bacin* a canal, where water is constantly running during the roasting. The *bacin* has at its bottom an opening, through which the quicksilver separated by the fire-action escapes into a cavity in a sewer connected to a reservoir, called *desazogadera*, where the condensed quicksilver resulting from the roasting operation is collected.

An iron piece, called *candelero*, is placed into the *bacin*; said *candelero* consisting of a ring, a disk with a hole in its centre, both parts secured by four iron rods. The *candelero* is situated so that the disk overtops the floor. Over said disk another one is placed, likewise bored in its centre, and called *platillo*. On the latter are placed the metal bars, alternating their edges, and forming a hollow centred cylinder called *piña*, which is covered by a cast-iron, brass, or copper bell, carefully packing with moistened ashes the joints between the bell and the *bacin*. Then the bell is wrapped up with long bricks, leaving a hollow space to be filled with coal, so that the fire may come in contact with the bell. Then the fire is kindled, and kept burning during ten or twelve hours. After allowing the bell to cool itself, the cover is taken away, and the metal bars are found unmelted, but free from quicksilver, provided the operation be successful. In order to be sure of it, any moist body, for instance, a piece of iron or wood, is approached to the bars. Should the roasting be imperfect, some quicksilver vapors will condense on the moist body, showing that the operation ought to go on.

Extraction of Polvillos. — Both on scraping the *arrastres* and on washing the amalgam, a certain amount of fine sand is obtained, containing variable quantities of silver, especially argentine pyrites, a great deal richer in gold than the ground ore. The separation of those metallic parts is performed by means of certain concentrating apparatus, called *planillas*, variable in their form; the more usual ones being boxes with declivious bottoms, about two metres long by one metre wide. On the upper part of said boxes the ore to be concentrated is placed; throwing to it some water, which drags down the terreous substances, leaving the powder on the upper part, although mixed with different substances. To get their complete purification, it is necessary to again and again wash the residue.

A certain quantity of the *pella* — escaped from the washing-vats when discharging them, or from the troughs when purifying the cake — is likewise obtained. The concentrated portions are called *polvillos* (fine powder), which are ground again in the *arrastre*, and calculated to be used instead of *magistral;* or are first calcinated, and afterwards ground, in order to extract from them a part of the gold and silver they contain. As much as two per cent of the ore richness is generally gotten out of the *tortillas*, although said rate may vary according to the kind of ore.

Results obtained from the Reduction. — The amount of silver extracted from the cake, added to the one settled on the *arrastres* bottom, is never equivalent to the amount indicated by the assays of the ground ore. There is always a loss, amounting in normal circumstances to five or eight per cent; it being also noticed, that, for each silver mark obtained, ten or twelve pounds of quicksilver are wasted.

Of the amount of gold indicated by the assay of the ground ore, seventy-five per cent is gotten when gold is pure, and no more than forty per cent, even less, when in pyrites.

Approximate cost of reducing thirty-two hundred weight of ore (one monton), the price of Indian corn being $1.37 a fanega, and $15½ cents the price of twenty-five pounds of straw. —

Crushing.

Food for 8 mules, per week	$10 00
4 laborers	13 50
1 driver	5 00
Wear and tear	4 00
Wages on 6 nights' work	19 00
	$51 50

which, divided by 56.25 *montones* generally crushed in one week, with 24 hours as daily work, gives, as cost per one *monton* $0 92

Grinding.

Food for 130 mules, at 18¾ cents per day, 7 days	$170 62½
1 foreman	13 00
1 second foreman	7 00
3 men for the hopper, at $3.00	9 00
5 men for the *arrastres*, at $4.00	20 00
3 watchmen, at $4.00	12 00
2 yard-keepers, at $3.00	6 00
1 man at the well	3 00
170 broom flags	10 62½
13 runner stones, at $2.50	32 50
	$283 75

which, divided by 56.25 *montones*, gives for each one of them 5 04

Yard.

25 mules to stir 100 *montones*:		
Mules	$4 68¾	
7 laborers	3 50	
Per *monton*, 8 cents, stirring 14 times	$1 12	
125 ℔ salt	2 50	
13 lbs. sulphate, at $12 per hundred weight	1 56	
1 foreman	$5 00	
2 watchmen	10 00	
	$15 00	
Say to 1 *monton*	0 28	$5 46

Washing, Purifying, and Roasting.

10 mules, 4 days	$7 50	
Sundry expenses	38 00	
8 hundred weight coal, at 75 cents	6 00	
	$51 50	
Say to a *monton*		0 51

General Expenses.

Wages	$65 00	
Rent	25 00	
Wear and tear and sundries	25 00	
	$115 00	
To 1 *monton*		2 22
Cost of reducing 1 *monton*		$14 15

REDUCTION OF ORES.

The *patio* process, invented by the miner of Pachuca, says Humboldt, "is one of those chemical operations which for centuries have been practised with a certain degree of success, notwithstanding the persons who extract silver from ores by means of mercury have not the smallest acquaintance either with the nature of the substances employed, or the particular mode of their action. The *azogueros* speak of a mass of ores as of an organized body, of which they augment or diminish the natural heat. Like physicians, who in ages of barbarism divided all ailments and all remedies into two classes, hot and cold, the *azogueros* see nothing in ores but substances which must be heated by sulphates if they are too cold, or cooled by alkalies if too warm."

SILVER: SYSTEM OF "BENEFICIATING" EMPLOYED (1880).

STATES.	PATIO. Kilograms.	TONEL. Kilograms.	LIXIVIACION. Kilograms.	FUEGO. Kilograms.	Total Kilograms Pure Silver.
Zacatecas	109,076 412	— —	— —	8,341 449	117,417 861
Guanajuato	104,310 530	— —	— —	1,001 091	105,311 621
Hidalgo	46,390 335	20,840 170	— —	28,271 478	95,501 983
San Luis Potosi . . .	30,322 306	— —	— —	37,516 555	67,838 861
Jalisco	34,222 216	— —	— —	— —	34,222 216
Sonora	28 974	— —	14,207 727	18,680 348	32,917 049
Durango	15,800 123	— —	— —	12,734 574	28,534 697
Chihuahua	8,619 534	— —	1,900 044	17,406 380	27,925 958
Sinaloa	5,551 168	— —	— —	6,153 847	11,705 015
Mexico	3,147 353	— —	— —	5,762 262	8,909 615
Michoacan	2,693 645	— —	— —	3,382 358	6,076 003
Oaxaca	121 721	3,663 673	— —	24 850	3,810 244
Guerrero	— —	— —	— —	2,005 612	2,005 612
Puebla	— —	— —	— —	712 991	712 991
Queretaro	— —	— —	— —	230 872	230 872
Amount	360,284 317	24,503 843	16,107 771	142,224 667	543,120 598

RÉSUMÉ.

```
                                           Kilograms.
By patio . . . . . . . . . . . . . . . . . 360,284 317
By tonel . . . . . . . . . . . . . . . . .  24,503 843
By lixiviacion . . . . . . . . . . . . . .  16,107 771
By fire . . . . . . . . . . . . . . . . . 142,224 667
```

Mining Nomenclature.—The following translations will be found to contain most of the terms in general use about mines in Mexico. Assessments, exhibiciones; assay, ensaye; a claim, pertenencia; blast, cohete; boiler, caldera; crosscut, crucero; croppings, creston; drain, desaguar; drill-hole, barreno; dividends, dividendos; dump pile, terreros; drill, taladro; dip of ledge, echada; engine, máquina de vapor; extension, próroga; front wall, respaldo alto; foot wall, respaldo bajo; gold, oro; hand-drill, barrena; hoisting whim, malacate; iron, hierro; locating, denuncio; mill and works, hacienda; mine corners, mojoneras; mine, mina; ore, metal; powder, pólvora; pump, bomba; quicksilver, azogue; shaft, tiro; silver, plata; slag, escorias; shareholders, accionistas; steam drill, perforador; tunnel, socavon; ton, tonelada; vein, veta; arroba, 25 pounds; quintal, 100 pounds; carga, 300 pounds; monton, 3,000 pounds; marco, about $8.85; metro, 39.37 inches; vara, 2 feet 9 inches.

Laborers in an Ordinary Mine, and their Average Wages (weekly). — 1 administrador, $25.00; 1 rayador, $6.00; 2 mineros, at $6.00; 1 capitan de patio, $5.00; 1 bartolinero, $4.00; 1 portero, $3.50; 2 fierreros, at $3.50; 3 veiadores, at $3.50; 12 destajeros (by the job), at $30.00.

Day Laborers. — Barrateros rayados, 62 cents; peones, 50 cents; manteros, 75 cents; paleros, $1.00; cajoneros, 87 cents; contras, 50 cents; arreadores, 37 cents; quebradores, 37 cents; carretoneros, 40 cents; corraleros, 31 cents; garraferos, 31 cents.

COINAGE OF THE MEXICAN MINTS.

The mint of Mexico was established in 1535, fourteen years after the capture of the Aztec city, under the first viceroy sent out from Spain.

The most careful estimates, in 1876, placed the total coinage at nearly $3,000,000,000 : —

	SILVER.	GOLD.
In the colonial period (1537 to 1821)	$2,082,260,657	$68,778,411
Since the independence (1822 to 1875)	787,055,080	47,327,383
Coinage of copper	5,272,855	
And we have up to 1875, in copper, silver, and gold		$2,990,694,386

The average annual coinage was at that time (1876) estimated at $20,500,000.

For ten years, this would be $205,000,000; making total coinage to 1885, $3,195,694,386.

That this estimate is not exaggerated, we are convinced by the actual returns for the economic year 1879, taken from the government statistics, and presumably accurate : —

COINAGE FOR THE YEAR ENDING JUNE 30, 1879.

MINTS.	GOLD.	SILVER.	COPPER.	TOTAL.
Mexico	$304,500 00	$5,116,000 00	$14,800 00	$5,435,300 00
Zacatecas	50,111 00	4,597,939 50	— —	4,648,050 50
Guanajuato	212,158 00	3,740,403 75	— —	3,952,561 75
San Luis Potosi	— —	2,519,110 00	— —	2,519,110 00
Guadalajara	3,830 00	1,413,161 00	1,500 00	1,418,491 00
Chihuahua	— —	806,025 00	— —	806,025 00
Culiacan	49,230 00	891,951 00	— —	941,181 00
Durango	23,935 00	854,882 50	— —	878,817 50
Alamos	13,700 00	756,598 15	— —	770,298 15
Hermosillo	1,360 00	555,650 00	— —	557,010 00
Oaxaca	3,700 00	153,610 00	— —	157,310 00
	$662,524 00	$21,405,330 90	$16,300 00	$22,084,154 90

RÉSUMÉ.

Gold	$662,524 00	
Silver	21,405,330 90	
		$22,067,854 90
Copper cents (*centavos*)		16,300 00
Total coinage in the year (economic) of 1879		$22,084,154 90

COINAGE.

Old Coinage.

Onza de oro (gold ounce) . . 16 dollars = £3.04
Media onza ó doble pistola . 8 " = 1.12
Pistola (one-fourth *onza*) . 4 " = 0.16
Escudo de oro (gold *escudo*), 2 " = 0.08
Escudito de oro . . . . . 1 " = 0.04
Peso fuerte de plata (silver dollar) . . . . 1 " = 0.04
Toston (silver half of a dollar), 4 reales = 0.02
Peseta (silver quarter of a dollar) . . . . 2 " = 0.01
Real (silver eighth of a dollar), 12½ cents = 6¼d.
Medio real (silver sixteenth of a dollar) . . . . . . 6½ "

Old Coinage — Continued.

Cuartilla (silver thirty-second of a dollar), 3 cents.
Tlaco (copper), half of a *cuartilla*.

New Coinage.

Gold 20 *pesos* . . . . 20 dollars = £4.0
Piece of 10 *pesos* . . . . 10 " = 2.0
Piece of 5 *pesos* . . . . . 5 " = 1.0
Silver 1 (10 *dineros* 20 *granos*), 1 " = 0 4
A half, 50 *centavos* . . . . . 50 cents = 0.2
A quarter, 25 *centavos* . . . 25 " = 0.1
A tenth, 10 . . . . 10 "
A twentieth, 5 . . . . 5 " = 2½d.
Copper 1 . . . . 1 " = ½d.

Nickel coins, in 1, 2, 3, and 5 cent denominations, were issued in 1883, but did not meet with favor from the people, who preferred silver.

WEIGHTS AND MEASURES.

Weights.

1 *onza*   (8 *ochavos*)   = 1   ounce.
1 *marco* (8 *onzas*)   = 0½   pound.
1 *libra* (2 *marcos*)   = 1   pound.
1 *arroba* (25 *libras*)   = 25   pounds.
1 *quintal* (4 *arrobas*) = 100   pounds.
1 *carga* (3 *quintals*) = 300   pounds.
1 *fanega* (140 pounds)   = 2   bushels, nearly.
1 *alumer* (*almuerza*)   = 0¹/₁₂ of a *fanega*.
1 *frasco*   = 5   pints, nearly.

Measures.

1 foot measures 0.928 foot English.
1 *vara* (3 feet Mexican) equals 2.784 feet English, or 2 feet 9.3141 inches English.
1 league (26.63 to 1 meridian) equals 5,000 *varas*, or 2.636 miles English.

New Measures.

Kilómetro (kilometre) equals 1,000 metres or 1,086 yards.
Metro (metre) equals 100 centimetres, or 1 yard 3½ inches.
Centimetro (centimetre) equals 2½ hundredths to an inch.

The metric system is legal in Mexico, and coming into general use, as it should be in the United States also, insuring uniformity in weights and measures throughout the continent.

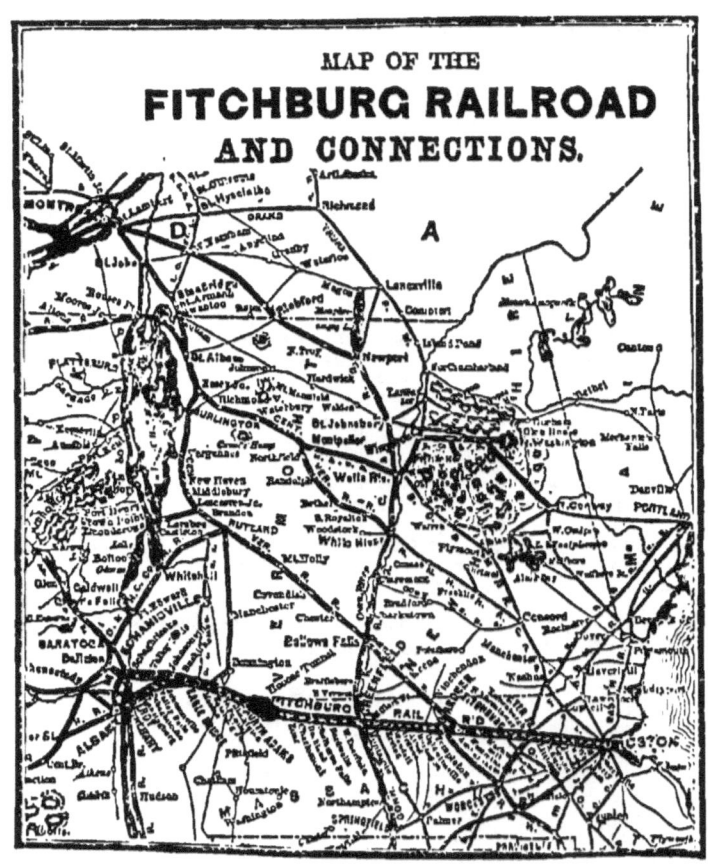

THE FAVORITE FAST TRAINS OF THE

Fitchburg Railroad

(Hoosac Tunnel Route)

TO ALL POINTS WEST

Are equipped with New and Elegant Pullman

PALACE DRAWING-ROOM & SLEEPING CARS.

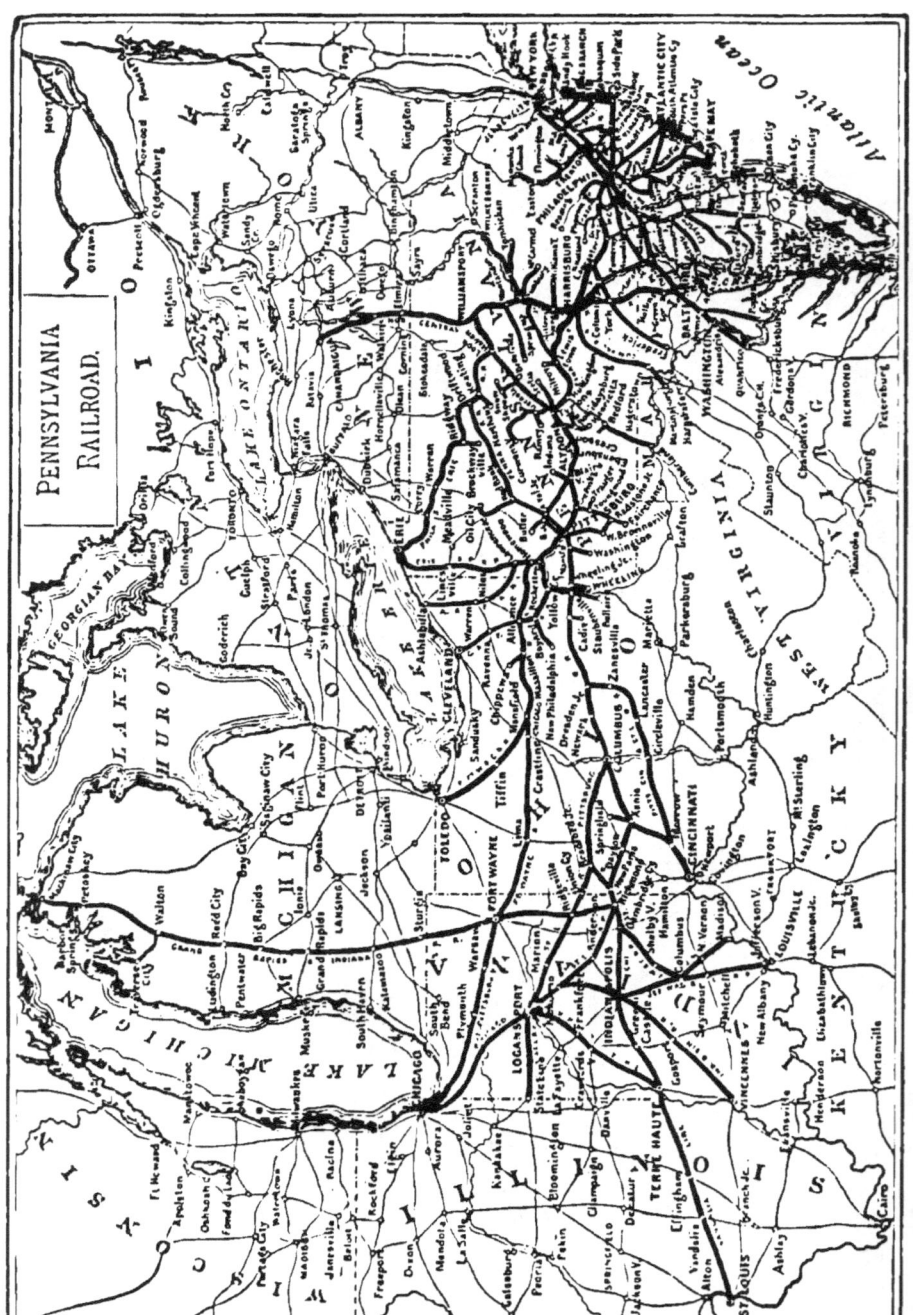

A GUIDE TO MEXICO.

ROUTE I.

From.	To.	Distance.	Time.
Boston	City of Mexico	3,883 miles.	172 hours.
New York	City of Mexico	3,730 miles.	162 hours.
Chicago	City of Mexico	2,871 miles.	134 hours.
St. Louis	City of Mexico	2,665 miles.	126 hours.

SPECIMEN TIME-TABLES.

(A) BOSTON, via CHICAGO, TO CITY OF MEXICO.

ROUTES:

```
              Eastern time.                                                    Central time.
Leave Boston     8.30 A.M. (Hoosac Tunnel Route) . . . . . arr. Chicago        6.45 2d P.M.
  "   Boston     6.00 P.M. . . . . . . . . . . . .   "    Chicago             8.00 2d A.M.
  "   Chicago   12.30 P.M. (Burlington Route) . . . . .   "    Kansas City    9.00    A.M.
                                                                              Mountain time.
  "   Kansas City 10.00 A.M. (via Atchison, Topeka, & Sta. Fé),   "  El Paso  4.30 3d P.M.
  "   El Paso    6.30 P.M. (Paso del Norte 7.15) . . . . . .  "  City of Mexico 7.10 3d A.M.
```

(B) BOSTON, via ST. LOUIS, TO CITY OF MEXICO.

ROUTES:

```
Leave Boston     3.00 P.M. (Hoosac Tunnel Route) . . . . arr. St. Louis   8.20 2d A.M.
  "   St. Louis  9.00 P.M. . . . . . . . . . . . . .  "  Kansas City     9.00   A.M.
  "   Kansas City for El Paso, etc., as in (A).
```

(C) BOSTON AND NEW YORK, TO CITY OF MEXICO.

ROUTES:

```
Leave Boston about 6.00 P.M. . . . . . . . . . . . . arr. New York      7.00    A.M.
  "   New York   (Pennsylvania Railroad) 8.00 A.M. . . . . .  "  St. Louis     7.30 2d P.M.
  "   St. Louis   9.00 P.M. . . . . . . . . . . . . .  "  Kansas City   9.00    A.M.
  "   New York   9.00 A.M. (New York and Chicago, Limited) . "  Chicago       10.30   A.M.
  "   New York   8.00 P.M. (Hotel Car, Pennsylvania Railroad)  "  Chicago     7.50 2d A.M.
  "   Chicago   12.30 (Burlington Route) . . . . . . . .  "  Kansas City    9.00    A.M.
  "   Kansas City 10.00 A.M. . . . . . . . . . . . . .  "  El Paso        4.30 3d P.M.
  "   El Paso    6.30 P.M. . . . . . . . . . . . . . .  "  City of Mexico 7.30 3d A.M.
```

NEW YORK AND ST. LOUIS, TO CITY OF MEXICO.

In selecting an Eastern road over which to travel westward, and eventually to connect with the vast system now opened into Mexico, one cannot do better than to take one, which from its length, its perfect road-bed, its double track, its steel rails, its fine rolling-stock, and its completeness of organization, should be a most desirable highway for the oncoming Mexican travel.

THE PENNSYLVANIA RAILROAD

had its actual beginning in the year (1846) that first heard the muttered thunders of the Mexican war; and from its humble inception, as a tributary to the canal system of Pennsylvania, it has grown to a magnitude almost beyond belief. The tracks of its main and leased lines would, it is said, if extended, reach from Philadelphia across the Atlantic, and through Europe to China. The steel and iron used in its rails and rolling-stock would make, if wrought into a single mass, a shaft eight inches in circumference, and 25,000 miles in length. Over its 7,000 miles of owned and leased lines roll 1,100 engines, and 1,100 passenger-cars, while 25,000 well-drilled employees work in the interests of this great corporation, the earnings of which are said to amount to $1,000 an hour.

Leaving New York at eight A.M., the special St. Louis train speeds through a country famous in continental history, — Newark, Trenton, Philadelphia, — and takes one over the richest agricultural region of Pennsylvania. Beyond Harrisburg, crossing the Susquehanna, it enters the spurs of the Alleghanies; later, winds through the valley of the Blue Juniata, passing such picturesque spots as Lewiston, Tyrone, Sinking Springs, and Altoona; and at Kittanning Point, 242 miles from New York, the great road winds around that wonder of engineering skill, the Horseshoe Curve. At Allegrippus "the majesty of the mountains seems to culminate," and beyond, the great tunnel is entered, over 2,000 feet above the sea, by which the crest of the Alleghanies is pierced, and, emerging from it, the descent is commenced toward the plains of the Great West. At the western base of the Alleghanies are numberless attractive resorts, as Conemaugh, Johnston, and the Pack-saddle Narrows, where the road threads the mountain-gorges amidst peerless scenery; and at Pittsburgh, the city of coal and iron, the Pennsylvania trunk-line terminates. But its influence is felt a thousand miles beyond, and the wise policy of its founders in early leasing and assisting new lines into the then unknown West is seen in the light of to-day, which shows that its projectors builded even better than they knew, and laid the foundation for a vast, and almost endless system, which penetrates the entire region of the great South-west, and whose eastern portal now stands open as the gateway to Mexico. Crossing Ohio, Indiana, and Illinois, the train finally reaches St. Louis at 7.30 of the evening of the second day from New York. In the great Union Depot, transfer is made by merely stepping from track to track, and taking a car of the Chicago and Alton, or the Missouri Pacific, at nine P.M.; and, after a comfortable night in the "sleeper," one arrives in Kansas City at nine in the morning. Another change is made here in the fine Union Depot, and an hour later, at ten, one is settled for a ride of fifty-four hours and 1,157 miles, which can be made without leaving the car, until the Rio Grande, the Mexican boundary, is reached.

DRAWING-ROOM CAR, PENN. R.R.

From Chicago (where change is made in Union Depot for cars of the Burlington Route) the time is about twenty hours to Kansas City, where connection is completed with the Atchison, Topeka, and Santa Fé Railroad.

Just thirty years ago, the Rev. E. E. Hale wrote, in a little book on Kansas, " There is not at this moment (Aug. 1, 1854) *a town or village of whites* in Kansas or Nebraska." Were this not history, it would seem most incredible, in view of the present condition of this great and flourishing State, with its thousands of churches and schoolhouses, its cities and progressive population.

The belief of this talented writer, that "the Territory of Kansas, from its position, is the great geographical centre of the internal commerce of the United States," was shared in, at a later period, by other intelligent citizens of Boston; and it is to the foresight of these men that the Atchison, Topeka, and Santa Fé, and the Mexican Central railroads, form one great system, extending from the Missouri River to the Aztec capital, a distance of over 2,300 miles. It was some seventeen years ago that a few enterprising men interested themselves in the railroads of Kansas, then in their infancy; but it was considered a great risk even to build the road which was to connect the Missouri River with Topeka. But these few capitalists evolved from chaos a liberal and successful corporation: "the infant soon became a giant," and has been the most important factor in the settlement and development of that vast country lying between the two great rivers, the Missouri and the Rio Grande. It has lent a helping hand to the farmers of the prairies of Kansas, the stock-men on the plains of Colorado, and the miners in the mountains of New Mexico. To every business, to every industry, this beneficent corporation extended aid, and while its engines chased the Indian and the buffalo from the fertile prairies, and spanned the arid wastes of desert, the settlers who followed in the wake of its engineers were encouraged to build homes, to erect schools and churches; and thus it is that along this road we see thrift and enterprise, and a New-England spirit of culture in its population. No road in this country has proved so beneficial to its supporters, and has so carefully provided for the comfort of its patrons. From its source to its ending, it has built elegant stations, and at convenient intervals provided commodious and comfortable hotels and dining-halls, at each of which a full half-hour is allowed for the discussing of a long and varied *ménu*.

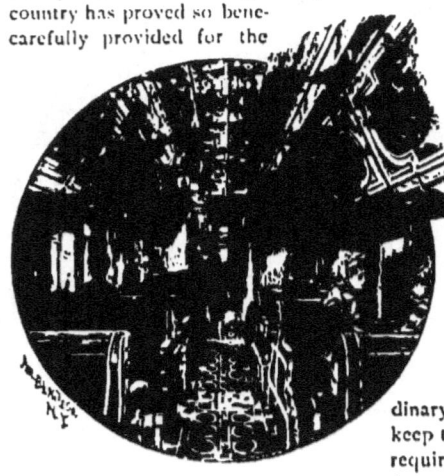

SLEEPING-CAR, PENN. R.R.

This great road, with nearly 2,000 miles of track, its hundreds of cars and engines, and thoroughness of equipment for the safety and comfort of passengers, is most wisely controlled by young and enterprising men, whose extraordinary penetration and grasp of affairs keep this gigantic corporation *ahead* of the requirements of the age. Although an independent and totally distinct corporation, yet its animating spirit is in harmony with that which pervades the great Pennsylvania Road; for likewise it has constantly encouraged the building of tributary lines, until its iron fingers extend over half a dozen great States and Territories, and progress and civilization follow as surely in its wake, as fertility the rill from the river in a desert region.

But for the settled purpose of the writer of these pages, not to diverge until the goal is reached (the City of Mexico), Kansas, with its numerous streams, its illimitable prairie ranches, its prosperous towns, growing so rapidly that their aspect constantly changes, would stop us to wonder a hundred times.

A road of the same standard gauge as those in the East, solid and smooth, conducts us across the entire length of Kansas. From the time we leave the union depot at Kansas City, until farewell is said to the United States at El Paso, there is a constantly shifting series of views, — "prairie, plain, plateau, peak, and pueblo." At Lawrence, as the train speeds by, one can see the noble buildings of the University of Kansas looking down upon the "most beautiful city of the West," — an historic city, for here was the first free-state settlement, and here began the great antislavery struggle. "It is peaceful enough now; but it numbers among its citizens men who stood shoulder to shoulder with John Brown, or looked into the barrels of Quantrell's rifles." Not far off is Topeka, a bright and enterprising city of 25,000, beyond which the road dips southward, and reaches the valley of the Arkansas, keeping the great river company nearly the entire breadth of the State, through scenery which in springtime may be called the fairest in the West. At Coolidge the road leaves Kansas, and at La Junta takes a departure from the Arkansas, and strikes southward, across a corner of Colorado, and enters New Mexico. Passengers from Pueblo, Colorado Springs, Denver, Leadville, and even from Salt Lake City and far-off San Francisco, can join the

CHICAGO TO MEXICO.

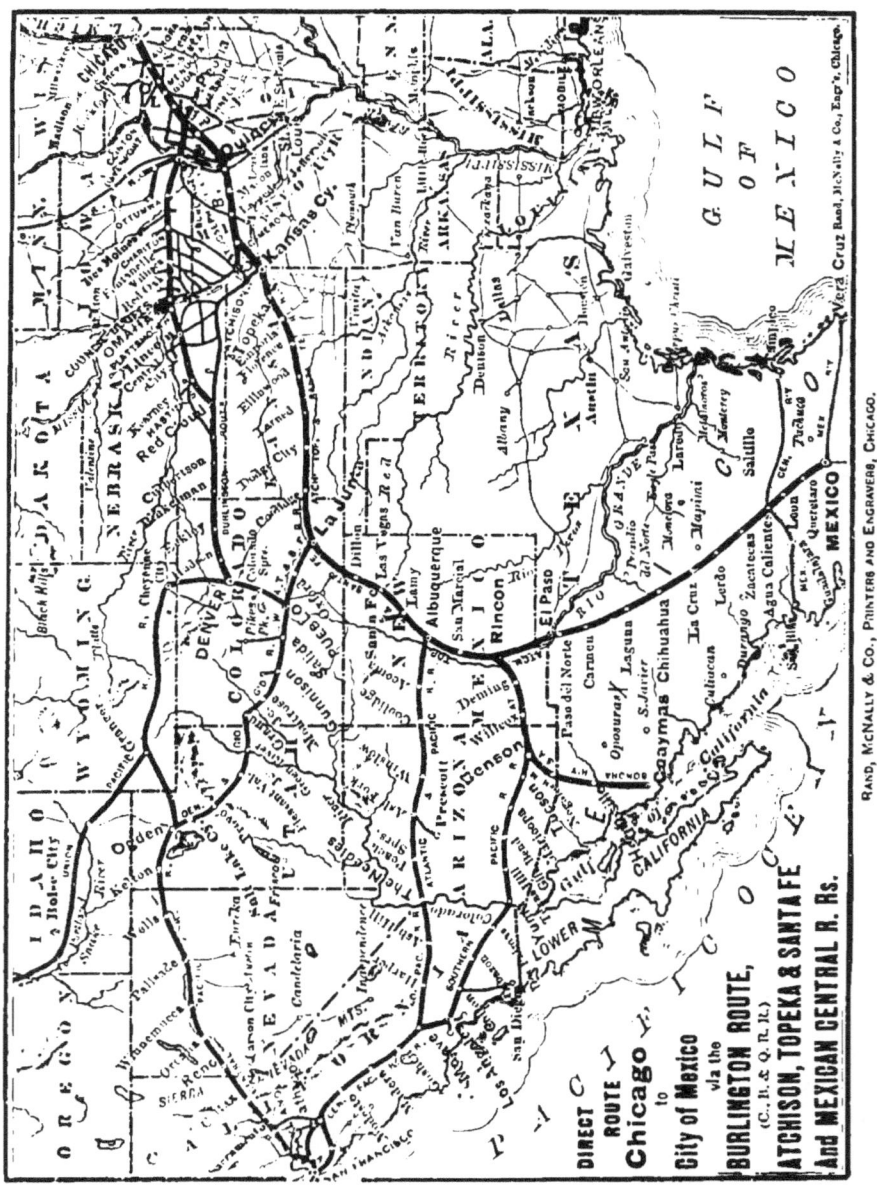

train at La Junta, and continue on into old Mexico, for here the wonderful Denver and Rio Grande Railroad comes down from its mountain fastnesses, and unites the "Central Pacific" system with the Atchison, Topeka, and Santa Fé.

ON THE SANTA FÉ TRAIL.

IN NEW MEXICO

we find ourselves entering territory once pertaining to the Mexican Republic, a portion of that New Spain obtained for the Spanish crown through the prowess of Cortés, and described by Humboldt. Here we shall more particularly observe the country — for it is radically different from Kansas and Colorado — and the people and architecture, which are alike strange and interesting. Almost rectangular in shape, the territory of New Mexico has an area of 121,200 square miles, and contains a population of 130,000 whites, about 8,000 Pueblo, and nearly as many more nomadic Indians.

From the time of our entrance into the territory, we shall observe a varied and wonderful landscape, — high and rugged mountains, as at Raton Pass, most picturesque *mesas* or table-lands, deep cañons, and wide-stretching plains. The mountains are covered with timber, the plains destitute of trees, while in the valleys, by means of irrigation, are raised bountiful crops of the fruits and vegetables of the temperate zone. From the mountains, which are spurs of the Rockies, and are reputed rich in ores of silver, copper, iron, and gold, come down the streams produced by the melting snows, but for which the plains of the northern portion of New Mexico would be but arid wastes. Chief of these is the Rio Grande, a turbid river, which has been called the Nile of America, as its waters have fertilized so many lands, and which, nearly 1,500 miles in length, after crossing the territory, forms the entire boundary line between Texas and Mexico. Although much has been claimed for New Mexico in the way of natural wealth, we cannot affirm that it possesses any greater attraction than its climate, which is indeed a glorious one, filling the year with bright, sparkling days, and making it an elysium for people afflicted with bilious disorders or pulmonary complaints. At no place in New Mexico — or, in fact, in the great South-west — is there such a sanitarium of nature's own creating, aided by man's efforts, as at the Hot Springs of Las Vegas, reached at a point 125 miles south of the Colorado line, and 777 miles west of Atchison, among the foothills of the Spanish mountains. More than a score of thermal springs lie hidden in a little valley, protected on every side from the penetrating winds that sometimes sweep the bleak plains. They contain sulphate

LAS VEGAS HOT SPRINGS.

and chloride of sodium, with traces of iodine, bromine, and lithium, while the bog through which their waters have for centuries percolated yields that curious silt used in the "mud baths" so efficacious in the treatment of cutaneous diseases.

In this mountain valley a great hotel was erected, a few years ago, at an expense of nearly a quarter of a million dollars, containing 250 rooms, heated by steam, and lighted with gas, with numerous appointments for the comfort of guests, and such sanitary provisions, that it was declared to be "a most delightful resting-place on the southern route across the continent." Baths in every variety — medicated, electrical, Turkish, vapor, with sprays and douches — are administered by experienced medical attendants, while all the establishments in this miniature Saratoga are supplied with water from the mountain-springs above, pure as the air which fills the lungs, and brings tonic to the systems of patients who seek here the fountain of rejuvenescence. The first hotel built here by the railroad company was destroyed by fire, in January, 1884, but it was soon rebuilt in a manner absolutely fireproof; and the second "Montezuma" awaits the coming of the health-seeker from every part of the United States. Above the springs and the hotels and cottages, a picturesque ravine leads far into the hills, toward cold mountain ponds, said to abound in trout, where the hillsides are covered with forests of pines, presumably the abode of game, and certainly delightful spots for the camper-out. The Arkansas valley, through which we passed in coming here, teems with certain game in the season; and all along the line, by branching off into the mountains, one may hunt for the red and black tail deer, mountain grouse and sheep, cinnamon and black bear, the plumed quail and wild turkey, and perchance come upon an elk, or a "mountain lion."

Every thing here is tonic and bracing; there are no enervating influences, such as counteract the benefits derived from the hot-springs and health-resorts of other States. A well-known physician, writing to a paper in Cincinnati, gives his opinion of these springs, as follows:—

MEXICAN ADOBE HUT.
(*Permission Missouri-Pacific Ry.*)

"The climate of Las Vegas is the general climate of the eastern slope of the Rocky Mountains, modified favorably by its sheltered position. At 6,767 feet above the sea-level they are more than a thousand feet higher than Denver, and three hundred feet lower than Santa Fé. They are nearly on a level with Manitou, and are seven hundred feet higher than Trinidad. The winters are mild. Snow rarely falls, and, when it comes, lies only three or four hours. Whole months go by in winter without rain or snow. Under a cloudless sky, with radiation unchecked by vapor, the nights are cool in summer, and positively cold in winter, yet the thermometer knows no zero, and, it is said, never touches 90° in summer. The annual rainfall is not more than twelve inches per annum, and a great portion of this is thrown down in July and August.

"It is impossible by words to give an idea of that sort of purity which the eye recognizes in the air of the plains and the mountains near. It is so translucent that distances are always amiss; the new-comer having no power to estimate by aerial perspective whether an object is five miles distant, or fifty. Its diathermancy is such, that one is never cold in direct sunlight. While it is certainly true that more light is received here per diem than in any portion of the United States, it is also true that there are more sunny days. From Denver to Santa Fé, at the broad and vague line where mountain and plain meet, there are only three or four days in each year whereon the sun does not shine. The clouds are few and the sun shows himself more than three hundred and sixty days in each year."

A short branch connects the main line with the Springs, turning off at the thriving town of Las Vegas; and sixty miles beyond, at Lamy, another branch diverges to the town of Santa Fé, about midway between which points the road passes within sight of the Pueblo of Pecos, the most ancient of Indian villages, and the traditional birthplace of one of the Montezumas.

Santa Fé is the oldest town within the present limits of the United States, containing the "oldest house in the country," "the oldest church," and a "palace," once the abode of Spanish viceroys. One of those sturdy pioneers who visited Santa Fé when under Mexican dominion, when only accessible by the dangerous "Santa Fé trail," declared that it resembled "a fleet of flatboats moored to a mountain;" and another has compared the *adobe* houses to "kilns of unburned bricks." With the exception of the stores around the plaza, and the houses of the wealthy, Santa Fé is mainly composed of mud huts, one-story *adobes*, built after the Mexican fashion, each around its central square, or *placita*, with clay floors, and flat clay roofs. The windows, until recently, — if any existed, — were oftener of mica than glass. There was little furniture: a bench of clay running around one side of the room formed a seat and bed, while the fireplace was in one corner. In fact, the dwellings of the natives of New Mexico are merely improved Indian houses such as are found throughout the border region of Mexico. The food, the religion, and customs of the people, are Mexican, not even excepting the decided preference for the *burro*, or donkey, as a means of conveyance.

One redeeming feature of Santa Fé is its large and handsome palace hotel, and another is its climate; while its ancient "cathedral" of San Miguel, a mud church built in 1590, and its other buildings savoring of antiquity, make up its list of attractions. The "tertio-millennial," or 333d anniversary of its first settlement, was most appropriately celebrated in 1883. Santa Fé's history is, however, sufficient of itself to attract hither numerous pilgrims, for its site was visited by Europeans within twenty years after the discovery of Mexico; and the soldiers of the adventurous Coronado here found a people quite as civilized as the Aztecs.

The native races, the Pueblos, — so called because they were found living in *pueblos* or villages, — were subjugated, but rebelled in 1680, and drove the Spaniards from the country, though they were again reduced to submission. In the early part of this century it was the objective point of the long caravans that wended their way thither from the far-distant Missouri, making the Santa Fé trail an historic feature of the South-west.

In 1848 New Mexico was annexed to the United States, becoming part of that country, though it still retains all the characteristics of a Mexican territory.

THE RAILROADS OF NEW MEXICO

at the opening of the year 1884 exceeded a total aggregate length of 1,100 miles, although not a single mile was in operation in 1880. Nearly 800 miles are controlled by the Atchison, Topeka, and Santa Fé, with 587 in its main line, and 200 in the Atlantic and Pacific. Nine hundred miles from the Missouri River is the flourishing town of Albuquerque, which, though its first buildings were erected in 1880, now contains 10,000 inhabitants, has five hotels, an opera-house, gas and electric lights, and expended $400,000 in new structures in 1883 alone. Here the St. Louis and San Francisco line crosses our path, the western division of which, the Atlantic and Pacific, forms the extension of the Atchison, Topeka, and Santa Fé system to California.

Could we diverge at this point from our direct journey into Mexico, we should penetrate a region yet more wonderful than that we have already passed over; we should discover ourselves in the heart of that country selected by the ancient Pueblos as their home; should pass such fascinating Indian towns as Isleta, Laguna, Acoma, with its village on a *mesa* 250 feet high, an impregnable fortress; at the station of Fort Wingate could take conveyance for Zuñi, which Mr. Cushing has made known to the world, or visit the great natural monument, the "Navajo Church," or Pyramid Rock, another titanic structure. Still beyond, a day's ride on horseback north, is the agency of Navajo Indians, skilled in agriculture and weaving. Twenty miles from the station of Holbrook is a petrified forest covering 1,800 acres, seventy miles north-west of which is Cataract Cañon, where a stream falls over a precipice 1,800 feet high; north of Winslow station are the curious Moquis Indians, and remarkable cliff-dwellings; at Cañon Diablo, on this line, is a bridge 540 feet long, spanning a chasm 225 feet deep; around Flagstaff are magnificent forests, with natural parks, where hunting and fishing may be found; and at Peach Springs one may leave the train, and penetrate to the heart of the Grand Cañon of the Colorado, twenty miles distant, through a gradually descending gorge called Diamond Wash, and behold the sullen waters of the imprisoned Colorado flowing between its mile-high walls of rock.

THE PUEBLOS.

We can take but a passing glimpse of those wonderful *adobe* structures of the semi-civilized Indians of New Mexico and Arizona, which prepare us for the more remarkable ancient buildings to be found in Old Mexico. Pecos lies near the line, between Las Vegas and Santa Fé, from which latter point may be reached Taos, and several others, less interesting; while near Wallace (where there is a good hotel) is a fine and typical pueblo, San Domingo; also at San Felipe, Isleta, and at various other points. To the average tourist, these remains of Indian civilization will doubtless prove more interesting than the modern towns, which are so rapidly growing into importance all along the great railroad.

At Rincon, 1,080 miles from the Missouri, the passenger for Sonora and the Gulf of California diverges from the main line, and at Deming, 1,149 miles, a place of remarkable growth, makes connection with the Southern Pacific Road to Benson (a busy mining-centre, 1,323 miles), whence the Mexico and Arizona and Sonora Railroads complete the distance to Guaymas, 1,676 miles. Objects of interest along this route are the mining-towns, as Tombstone and Contention; the plains of Sonora; the Mexican towns; the scenery about Hermosillo (1,586 miles), its Hill of the Bell, and lovely orange-gardens; and the magnificent harbor of Guaymas, whence steamers depart for the lower Mexican coast, and infrequent sailing-vessels for Lower California.

Running directly southward from Rincon, the Atchison, Topeka, and Santa Fé passes through scenery unrelieved by any notable objects, until El Paso is entered (1,157 miles), and the Rio Grande is reached, which separates the territories of the two republics. Here is a thriving and progressive town, born of railway activity, with good hotels, large stores, and excellent buildings. Four lines — the Texas-Pacific from the East; the Galveston, Harrisburg, and San Antonio from the South-east; the Southern Pacific from the West; and the Atchison, Topeka, and Santa Fé from the North — concentre here; all having fine stations, and valuable property. The scenery about is not interesting, though peculiar and pleasing; brown and detached ridges rising above plains dotted along the Rio Grande with trees and vineyards. The great river, here of varying breadth, according to the season, is spanned by substantial bridges, which connect with a Mexican town of ancient date, — Paso del Norte, founded two hundred years ago, and containing 5,000 inhabitants. The buildings of the Mexican Central are the finest in this place; but the old church, the *adobe* houses, the *acequias* (or irrigating canals), and the vineyards will attract attention. Change is made at El Paso; and the cars continue on into Mexico, over a road virtually an extension of the same system as the one just described.

THE RIO GRANDE, NEAR EL PASO.
(*On the Texas-Pacific Ry.*)

Southward from El Paso, 225 miles, lies the city of Chihuahua (Chee-wâh-wah), reached over a route through desolate sand-hills at first, and latterly a vast grazing ground. It is the capital of the State, and its only city of note, with about 18,000 inhabitants. Its houses are of a single story, as a rule, with thick walls, grated windows, and open courts, with rooms from twelve to eighteen feet in height. The city enjoys a delightful climate, rarely above 70° in the shade, the thick house-walls admirably protecting from extremes of heat and cold. Epidemics and fevers are unknown; the pure air is conducive to health and longevity. To the recently arrived Americans are due the many new industries of Chihuahua, which draws its supplies from the distant cities of the United States. A horse-railway connects the station with the town, a mile distant. Objects of interest: the great and handsome church, an old convent, the monument to Hidalgo, chapel of Guadalupe, the aqueduct (three and one-half miles long), the upper and lower *paseos*, the central plaza with its fine fountain, the market, public swimming-bath, reduction-works (near the city), the Santa Rosalia mines (six miles distant) which have yielded fabulously in the past, and the beautiful *hacienda* of Don Enrique Müller (two miles away). Hotels: United States, and American, three dollars per day.

Taking a direction southward, a little westerly, the railroad runs to a point on the Durango border-line, not far distant from a cluster of famous mining-villages. Halfway to the line, it passes near Santa Rosalia, where are some celebrated hot-springs. About a day's ride by diligence, west of the railroad at Huajuquilla, is Parral, a thrifty mining-town, with a flower-adorned plaza and a fair hotel.

The general character of the great plateau through Chihuahua, Durango, and Zacatecas, is sterile, and to the eye forbidding; and the lack of fuel and water will keep it so, though rich mines here and there have created prosperous towns. The plateau along which the railroad takes its course has not its like, probably, in the world, as it runs, without an important obstruction, from Santa Fé in New Mexico to the Aztec capital. The following altitudes illustrate this:—

Santa Fé, 7,047 feet above the sea; Paso del Norte, on Rio Grande, 3,815; Chihuahua, 4,273; Durango, 6,848; Fresnillo, 6,244; Zacatecas, 8,038; Aguas Calientes, 6,262; Lagos, 6,376; Leon, 6,000; Silao, 5,911; Guanajuato, 6,836; Salamanca, 5,761; Celaya, 6,017; Queretaro, 6,362; San Juan del Rio, 6,490; Tula, 6,733; Mexico, 7,469.

Off the line of road, in an obscure corner of Durango, is the small though rich town of Mapimi, famous for its mines of gold, silver, and lead. The capital of the State, Durango, lies to the westward of the road, with which it is connected by stages. It was founded by the Viceroy Velasco, in 1559, previous to which time it was a frontier post erected against the Northern Indians. It contains about 28,000 inhabitants, has regular streets, shaded walks, and plazas, watered by a large spring; some beautiful bridges span a fine stream; its cathedral is celebrated for its richness of ornament; its "palace" is large; its markets are excellent; its schools (eighty-nine in the State) are well cared for; its institute (*Instituto Juarez*) has 250 students; another (for girls), 150; and it has a *Montepio*, or government pawn-shop, like the City of Mexico. The climate of Durango is cool and healthy, the soil fertile in watered valleys, but generally sterile. A wild country stretches southward to Sombrerete, a great mining-town with 20,000 people, where in olden times bonanzas, the richest in America, have been extracted from its famous *veta negra*, or black vein, of silver. It lies on the old wagon-trail; but the railroad leaves it to the east, and at Fresnillo strikes another great mining-centre, with 28,000 population. The hills about this town are full of mines which have been rich, whatever their condition now. A share which the government once held in one yielded an annual revenue of $500,000; but Santa Anna when in power, eager to possess all the golden eggs at once, sold its interest for less than one year's income. Around Fresnillo, and north and east, to Catorce and San Luis Potosi, stretches a "waste and sterile moorland, almost treeless, with little natural vegetation save the mesquite, with only an occasional hacienda to be met with, and the people collected in the crowded mining-towns." Such is the approach to Zacatecas, capital of the State, with a population of 64,000. This populous city is in the midst of the richest mines of Mexico.

Zacatecas is a mountain country of the high plateau, cut up by spurs of the Cordillera, and mostly arid and inhospitable. The region between San Luis Potosi and Sombrerete, and Mazapil and Zacatecas, is a broad plain, interspersed with a few swelling knolls, and an occasional group of hills or mountains. The country is unusually dry; and water-tanks, wells, and reservoirs are important features of an estate, and noteworthy objects to the traveller in this arid region. Zacatecas, the capital, is situated at the foot of an abrupt and picturesque porphyritic mountain, upon the rugged summit of which is perched a neat church and a small fortress. Its streets are short and crooked; its public buildings, especially the mint, city-hall, and cathedral, are magnificent edifices. Hotels: Diligencias, Comercio, Zacatecano.

The hillsides are full of mines, and also the town itself; one having been opened in the Alameda. It is safe to say that Zacatecas will not attract the tourist any more than the uninviting cities Durango and Chihuahua, to the north of it; but to those who would study the processes by which the wealth of the Sierra Madre

FOUNTAIN AT CHIHUAHUA.
(*Engraved for Missouri-Pacific Ry.*)

is torn from the bosom of the vast mountain-chain, this and the other cities mentioned will ever be interesting.

About thirty miles to the south-west of the capital are the remarkable ruins of Quemada, on the *Cerro de los Edificios*, about five miles north of the town of Villanueva. These constitute one of the largest groups north of the Mexican Valley, and are supposed to indicate an Aztec resting-place during the long migration of that people southward.

From Zacatecas, it is 106 kilometres to Aguascalientes, capital of the State of that name, which formerly constituted a part of Zacatecas, more celebrated for its agriculture than for its mines. It is famous for the number of hot-springs which surround the town. These thermal waters, in fact, give the state and town its name, — Aguascalientes (hot water or springs). The city contains 35,000 inhabitants, and is well supplied with factories, schools, and colleges. A thriving city west of the railroad is San Juan de los Lagos, situated in a deep ravine, little above the surface of the river. It is mainly composed of mud huts; though its large and beautiful church, dedicated to "Our Lady of the Lake," is famous throughout the country. An annual fair is held here, lasting eight days, to which the people of the entire region resort, in December of each year.

Jalisco is a large and populous State, lying upon the western slope of the cordillera; and here the traveller will find the temperature sensibly increased, as contrasted with that of the cities and towns along the line, both north and south of it. It belongs, in fact, to the *tierra caliente*, — the hot country, — and is capable of producing all tropical productions, which might also be raised in the deep and hot ravines of the narrow section traversed by the railway. The portion of the plateau on the western declivity of the cordillera enjoys a more fertile soil and more temperate climate than that above, as evidenced by the populous towns of Lagos and Leon, which do not depend upon the mines, but upon the soil.

About thirty-six miles farther is the city of Lagos, containing 20,000 inhabitants, — a prosperous place. There is a church here, — larger than the one at San Juan, but with less costly decorations, — commenced in 1784.

Leon, thirty-six miles farther, lies about ten miles within the border of the State of Guanajuato, at an elevation above the sea of 6,000 feet, in a fine, highly cultivated valley dotted with fields of corn and wheat. It is well built, and has several large religious edifices, though with none so noteworthy as in the towns just passed. The plaza is a large and beautiful one, paved with cobble-stones in mosaic, and with an elegant fountain. The city-hall and public buildings are large and handsome. The climate here is temperate, ranging from 60° to 80° the year round. Oranges are cultivated here, though other tropical fruits do not flourish; and the flower-gardens of Leon are celebrated. Leon is 258 miles from the city of Mexico; and the event of its being placed in rail connection with the capital was celebrated with great rejoicings. It is celebrated for its factories, and is the market-town for an extensive agricultural district.

The next large town is Silao, "between which and Leon," says a traveller, before the advent of the railroad, "the eye looks in vain for signs of cultivation."

A branch line of fourteen miles connects Silao with the famous city of Guanajuato, capital of the State of the same name. This city, containing about 65,000 inhabitants, lies at an elevation above the sea of some 800 feet higher than the general altitude of the line of road; Leon being at 6,000, and Celaya, to the east, 6,020. It is built in so rugged a region, and is so securely hedged in by hills and mountains, that it was found impossible to run the main line to the capital city; hence the branch from Silao of twelve miles to the suburban town of Marfil, whence a tramway leads to the outskirts of the city itself. The inauguration of the opening of the Central Railroad to this point was celebrated on the 22d of November, 1882, with unusual splendor. A special excursion-train was run from Mexico, containing about 150 people, comprising many of the most distinguished men of the Republic. The streets were illuminated, the buildings decorated, and *fiestas* and fireworks gave expression to the joy of the people in having been at last brought into connection with the capital city. This town, says a well-informed writer, is, perhaps, the most curiously picturesque and remarkable in the Republic. "Entering a rocky cañada, the bottom of which barely affords room for a road, you pass between high *adobe* walls, above which, up the steep, rises tier above tier of blank, windowless, sun-dried houses, looking as if they had grown out of the earth. Every corner of the windings of this road is filled with buildings of mining companies; huge fortresses of stone, ramparted, as if for defence. The scene varies with every moment. Now you look up to a church with purple dome

INTERIOR OF MEXICAN HUT.

and painted towers; now the black *adobe* walls, with here and there a spicy cypress or graceful palm between them, rise far above you, along the steep ledges of the mountain; and again the mountain itself, with its waste of rock and cactus, is all you see. The cañada finally seems to close : a precipice of rock, out of a rift in which the stream flows, shuts the passage. Ascending this, by a twist in the road you are in the heart of the city."

"Guanajuato impressed us," says another, "with an idea of permanence and comparative prosperity rather unusual in this part of the country, in spite of its greatly reduced population, its languishing industries, and its suburban mining-towns deserted, and tumbling into ruins. It has many beautiful private residences, which cannot be excelled in comfort, extent, and elegance, in any part of the United States, and many still wealthy and aristocratic families of pure, or nearly pure, Castilian descent."

The reservoirs, substantial and beautiful structures thrown across a stream which flows above the city, furnish it with water; and terraced promenades around them are favorite resorts of the people.

"Above the city, not far from the reservoirs, is a peculiar high mountain crowned with a curious perpendicular rock, which, from its fancied resemblance to the outlines of a giant buffalo, has been christened 'El Buffa.' From this mountain is procured in unlimited quantities a species of beautifully variegated sandstone, of all the colors of the rainbow, blue, pale green, and chocolate predominating. The sandstone cuts readily, has a fine grain; and of this material residences have been constructed of the most beautiful style, lining the cañon all the way up to the reservoirs. Graceful pillars in long colonnades, arched portals and corridors, and patios decorated with all the flowers of this prolific climate, are seen by the delighted traveller on every side."

The mint here is said to be the best in Mexico, and one of the few run by steam; while the reduction-works, though mainly run on the old Mexican plan, are the most famous in the country. In the mountains northeast of the city is the wonderful mine of Valenciana, which has produced $800,000,000, and has been worked ever since the Conquest. No traveller can afford to miss Guanajuato since it has been rendered accessible by steam, if he would care to become informed upon the mining resources of the Republic. Guanajuato sustained a terrible part in the tragedy of the revolution; and the Castle of Grenaditas still stands to point out where many brave men perished. When in 1810 the patriot priest Hidalgo led his rabble of Indians to this city, the Spaniards intrenched themselves in this Castle of Grenaditas, where they bravely sustained a long siege. Finding it to be impossible to carry the fortress by storm, a brave Indian, it is said, took a great flat stone upon his back, and, unharmed by the bullets rained upon it from above, reached the castle-gates, and set them on fire. The garrison was put to the sword. The year following, Hidalgo was defeated by the Spanish commander, and, fleeing to Chihuahua, was captured and shot; and his head and the heads of his companions, brought here and hung up on four hooks, are still shown at the four corners of the castle. The victorious Calleja also took vengeance upon the inoffensive inhabitants of Guanajuato for harboring the insurgents, and slaughtered them without mercy, till the fountains of the city were choked with blood.

The region through which the road passes after leaving Silao is known as the BAXIO, "so celebrated in Mexico, both as the seat of the great agricultural riches of the country and the scene of the most cruel ravages of the civil war."

There are great plains here, in places dry and verdureless, but generally fertile and well cultivated. The ranchos are of large size; the haciendas being perfect fortresses, loop-holed and battlemented.

Irapuato, in the centre of this district, is an old market-town, with no notable buildings save its churches; then comes Salamanca, at 333 kilometres, and finally, Celaya, at 292 from Mexico. Great fields of corn, and some olive-orchards, indicate the fertility of the valleys now passed through. Celaya contains 30,000 inhabitants, and is a city of importance, with large factories and intelligent laborers. It is supplied with water at blood-heat, by an artesian well 400 feet deep; and in this place, and other manufacturing towns near, there is an abundant supply.

In the district of Guanajuato, said Mr. Evans, who travelled with the Seward party across Mexico in 1869-70, "within a circuit of fifteen miles there is estimated to be, at this time, $40,000,000 worth of silver ore which will yield $25 to the ton; but, owing to the expense of reducing it there, it will not pay for working at all, and is now lying valueless on the surface of the ground. A railroad of about a hundred miles, through a wonderfully rich valley, offering no engineering obstacles of any amount, would connect the two cities, and enable the builder to bag $20,000,000 in profits on this ore already out, to say nothing of the future."

Since this, the then unexpected event of a railroad has been realized, though not, probably, his sanguine prediction regarding the working of the silver waste. Two great railways pass through Celaya, as the Mexican National here crosses the Central on its route from San Luis Potosi to Acámbaro and Mexico. Celaya has twelve churches; while its principal factory cost, including machinery, $400,000.

QUERETARO is the first place in the State bearing the same name, and is 246 kilometres from Mexico. It contains 48,000 inhabitants. Queretaro has the reputation of being the loveliest to the eye of any city outside the valley of Mexico. The first object claiming attention, should you approach it from the south, would be its magnificent aqueduct, much finer and grander than the two which supply the city of Mexico. Its arches curve above columns 50 or 60 feet high, — so high that the whole structure has a light and graceful appearance. It was built by the Marquis de Valero del Aguila, at his own cost, during the reign of the viceroys. It is two miles in length, and 90 feet in height, and connects with a tunnel in the neighboring hills, bringing pure water to the city from a point five miles away. As Queretaro lies at an altitude of 7,000 feet above the sea, it enjoys a delightful and temperate climate, and is surrounded by the vegetation and fruits of the temperate zone. It is built upon, and is surrounded by, hills; and the views, both of and from the city, are exceptionally fine. Of the approach to the city, Bishop Haven writes: "The city ever allures us on. Its towers and domes glisten in the dying light, half hidden among abundant foliage. The hollow of the hills looks small from this height, and the city seems embossed on the bottom of a bowl of radiant green. A farther descent brings the aqueduct to view, — the stateliest Roman that is extant in America; and there is no grander in Italy, nor one so grand. The valley lies about you full of verdure: never did any valley look lovelier. Hundreds of acres of wheat and barley and lucern, greenest of the green, seem in a race for superiority in color; while the trees are not behind in beauty. Flowers of richest hue bloom in the gardens; and the city stands forth, with its glittering towers and domes, a spectacle long to be remembered. It would be hard to find the equal in beauty of this combination of high, bold cliffs, ranges of hills, velvet meadows, and stately churches."

There are cotton-mills here that may vie with those of Lowell, in size, and number of spindles and operatives. One, the "Hercules," employs 1,800 hands and 18,000 spindles. These cotton-factories, surrounded by large and beautiful gardens, where bloom rare flowers, and choice fruits ripen, are models of their class. They should be visited by every one desiring to witness the industry of the native Indian when regularly employed, and the effect of capital in the hands of enterprising Mexicans.

The alameda, or public garden, here is very pleasant; and there are many old convents and churches worthy a visit. An ancient city, on the site of one built by the former Indian inhabitants, Queretaro also has an added interest as being the scene of two important historical events. Here the treaty of peace between Mexico and the United States was finally ratified by the the Mexican Congress in 1848. Here, also, was sounded the death-knell of the empire of Maximilian, when that pseudo emperor lost his life. It is not necessary to recount the events of that month of May, 1867, when Maximilian, his forces surrounded by the invincible army of the North, sustained siege in this city of Queretaro. The Hill of Bells, *El Cerro de las Campanas*, south-west of the city, indicates the point at which Maximilian was captured, and where he was subsequently shot, in company with Miramon and Mejia. He had fortified the old convent of Las Cruces, an immense structure with massive walls; and here, later, he was confined, and from a cell in this building led out to be shot. Las Cruces is now in ruins; and the town, especially in the outskirts, still shows, in roofless houses and in the marks of cannon-balls, the ravages of the war. The streets of Queretaro are narrow and winding; the houses of stone, low, massive, and bright in color; and here and there are little plazas adorned with flowers and tropical shrubbery. Though not rich in mines, the State of Queretaro contains celebrated deposits of opals, not far from the capital. A rich and broad valley extends beyond, filled with productive cornfields. Passing through this, we reach, at a distance from the city of Mexico of 191 kilometres,

QUERETARO AND BEYOND.

the old and flourishing town of San Juan del Rio, celebrated for the beauty of its fields and gardens; even Humboldt mentioning them so long ago as 1803. Numerous churches and useless convents are found here; but there is little to claim attention. Beyond, are various small towns, such as Nopala; and at Tula, but eighty kilometres, or fifty miles, distant from Mexico, we enter a town older, probably, than any other on the line.

There are fair hotels here, as also at the various cities and towns now pierced by the railroad, with prices at about the average in the United States, with a trifle rougher style of accommodations. The charm of Tula consists chiefly in its antiquity. Not only has it an old cathedral — one of the very first built after the Conquest — and a massive bridge nearly as old; but it is half encircled by hills crowned with remains of very ancient structures. In the plaza are shown carved pillars; and tradition is very firm in the statement that Tula was the site of a Toltec city more than a thousand years ago. Lying on the northern verge of the valley of Mexico, on the banks of the River Tula, or Montezuma, the situation of the town is pretty, although the surrounding soil and vegetation are not rich. In fact, we have left behind us the fertile soil and the exuberant vegetation of the central Baxio, and are now in a different land, though on the same plateau. Cactus, agave, and upland palm adorn vast plains, uncultivated and lava-strewn; and in the fifty intervening miles to Mexico little of cultivation is seen.

We pass El Salto at sixty-two kilometres from the capital, and Huehuetoca at forty-seven, and enter that great cut through the mountain-ridge that hems in the valley of Mexico, the Tajo of Nochistongo, dug to drain the upper lakes.

The aspect of the valley of Mexico, as entered from any point of compass, is beautiful in a general way; but a nearer view will not impress one so favorably. The soil is sterile, denuded of attractive vegetation, and the surface worn into gullies, ravines, and barrancas, by repeated rains. Huehuetoca is a dismal, dreary, uninteresting place; and Cuautitlan, but twenty-seven kilometres from the capital, though populous, has nothing at all to attract a stranger. An exception may be made, however, in favor of its Sunday bull-fights, to which the roads run loaded trains, at great profit. In fact, no one would care to linger in the northern portion of the valley, between Tula and Mexico, except it were for the inspection of places made fascinating by historic events of world-wide renown. Zumpango is one of these points. It was the seat of a powerful Chichimec chief, before the coming of the Aztecs; and the lake here is the one that has caused most disaster from inundation to the city of Mexico. It lies eastward from the railroad, its waters sparkling in the clear sunlight of this great elevation above the sea.

If the region we have now entered be not so fruitful in returns to the agriculturist, it is a glorious field for the seeker after the picturesque and for the student of history. Though stripped of the forests that once gave it shade and fertility, yet the bare hills have a beauty peculiarly their own; and the almost numberless villages and haciendas, with white walls gleaming amongst fruit and flowering trees of garden and field, render the scene one long to be remembered. We have now come in sight of the great volcanoes, Popocatapetl and Iztaccihuatl, that keep watch and ward over the historic city of the Aztecs; and soon the intervening space is passed, and the long journey from El Paso, of 1,225 miles, is ended.

THE CITY OF MEXICO.

So much has been written of this city, the objective point of all tourists to Mexico, that whatever could be given now would be merely repetition;[1] and we will confine ourselves to an outline of its attractive points.

From the railroad-station at Buena Vista, horse-cars and coaches convey passengers to any part of the city, and are in waiting for all trains. For the convenience of visitors who will later wish to visit various portions of the city, the following list of hacks and prices is appended: —

HACK STANDS AND RATES.

No. 1, Seminario; No. 2, Puente de Palacio; No. 3, San Jose de Gracia; No. 4, Estampa de la Merced (vacant); No. 5, Segunda de Vanegas; No. 6, Plaza de Santo Domingo; No. 7, Celaya; No. 8, Mesones (vacant); No. 9, Tercer Orden de S. Agustin (vacant); No. 10, Mariscala; No. 11, Rosales; No. 12, Avenida Juarez; No. 13, Corpus Christi; No. 14, Gante; No. 15, Independencia; No. 16, Coliseo; No. 17, Refugio; No. 18, Hotel Gilow; No. 19, Calle de Vergara; No. 20, Hotel de S. Agustin; No. 21, Vizcainas (vacant); No. 22, Mercaderes; No. 23, San Jose el Real; No. 24, Empedradillo; No. 25, Manrique; No. 26, Hotel Bella Union; No. 27, Hotel Gran Sociedad; No. 28, Puente de la Leña; No. 29, Puente Québrado; No. 30, D. Juan Manuel; No. 31, S. Juan de Letran; No. 32, de S. Diego.

Hacks showing green flags are paid $1.50 per hour; blue, $1.00; red, 75 cents; white, 50 cents. Before six o'clock in the morning, and after nine o'clock at night, the above rates are doubled. On feast days, hack-drivers are paid as follows: green flag, $2.00; blue, $1.50; red, $1.00. Any misconduct on the part of cab-drivers should be reported to Antonio Meneses, on the first floor of the Municipal Palace.

STREET-RAILROADS TO SUBURBAN TOWNS.

San Angel, via Mixcoac. Cars leave Plaza de Armas and San Angel simultaneously, at 6 A.M., and every 80 minutes afterwards, except on Sunday, when they leave every 40 minutes. Fare: first-class, 25 cents; second-class, 12½ cents.

Mixcoac. San Angel cars. Fare: first-class, 18 cents; second-class, 9 cents.

Tacubaya, via Chapultepec. Cars leave Plaza de Armas at 5.20 A.M., and run every 20 minutes till 8 P.M. Fare: first-class, 12½ cents; second-class, 6¼ cents. Monthly commutation-tickets: first-class, $5.50; second-class, $3.50.

Atzcapotzalco, via Tacuba. Cars leave Plaza de Armas and Atzcapotzalco simultaneously, at 6 A.M., and every hour afterward till 8 P.M. Fare: first-class, 12½ cehts; second-class, 6¼ cents.

Tacuba. Atzcapotzalco cars. Fare: first-class, 10 cents; second-class, 6¼ cents.

Tlalpam. Cars leave Plaza de Armas and Tlalpam simultaneously, at 6, 7.30, 9, 10.30 A.M., 12 M., and 2, 3, 3.30, 5, and 6.30 in the afternoon. Fare: first-class, 31 cents; second-class, 18 cents.

Guadalupe. Cars leave Plaza de Armas at 5 A.M., and run every half-hour till 1.30 P.M., and from 2.45 P.M. to 7.45 P.M. Cars leave Guadalupe every half-hour,

---

[1] See the author's Travels in Mexico, Chaps. XII.-XVI., etc.

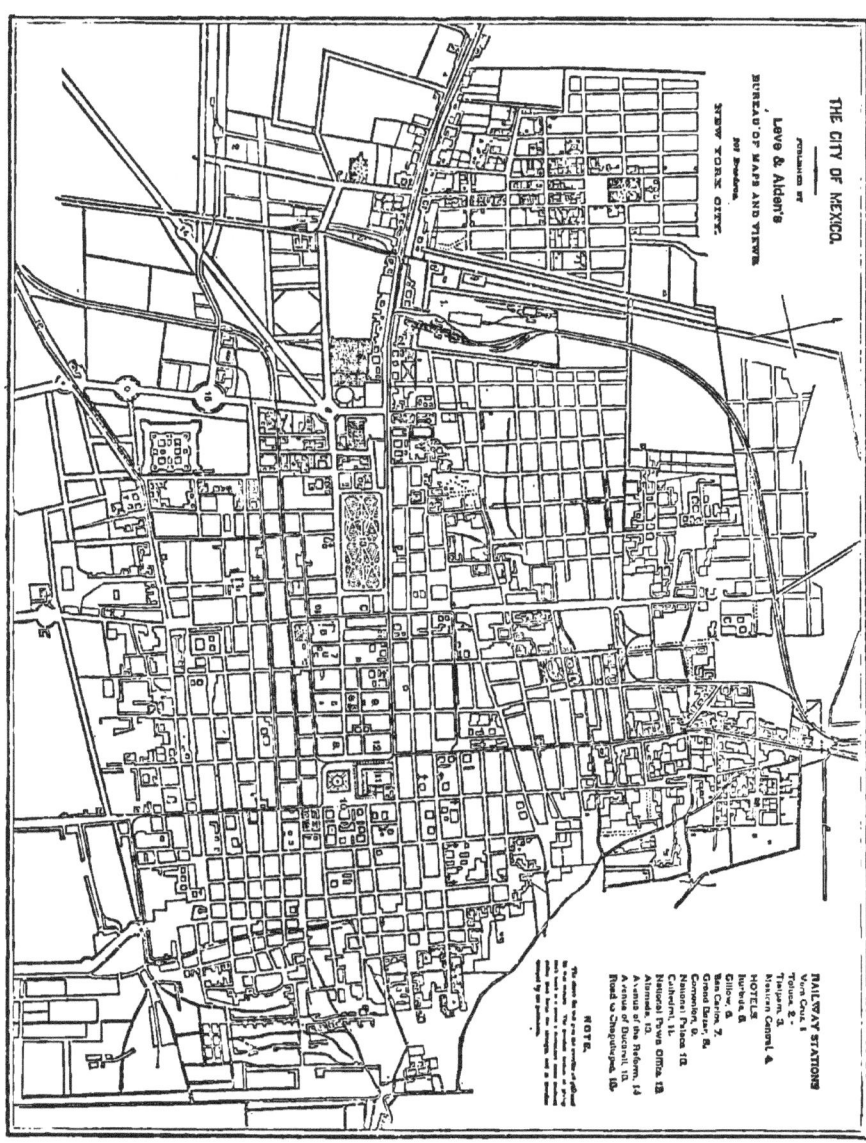

NEW YORK, HAVANA, VERA CRUZ.

Alexandre Steamship Line.

STEAMERS AT PRESENT

LEAVE NEW YORK EVERY THURSDAY
FOR
VERA CRUZ via HAVANA,
AND
LEAVE VERA CRUZ EVERY THURSDAY
FOR
NEW YORK via HAVANA.

Trip between New York and Vera Cruz about ten days, including stoppages at Havana, generally one or two days, at Progreso, Yucatan, about one day.

Steamers also stop every two weeks at

CAMPECHE and FRONTERA,

Making the trip, with these several stoppages, more like a

PLEASURE-EXCURSION.

The railway trip from Vera Cruz to the

CITY OF MEXICO

is considered

BEYOND COMPARISON,

The road being built up the mountain, and rising to an elevation of 8,000 feet.

The ever spring-like climate of the City of Mexico

CANNOT BE SURPASSED.

(See page 31 of "Guide.")

IN THE CITY OF MEXICO.

from 5.15 A.M. to 1.45 P.M., and at the same interval, from 2.30 to 8.30 P.M. Fare: first-class, 12½ cents; second-class, 6¼ cents.

La Viga. Cars leave Plaza de Armas every 15 minutes, from 6.45 A.M. to 8 P.M. Fare, 6¼ cents.

The street-car company that has charge of the suburban routes has cars for special occasions, the terms for which may be had by applying at the office in the Plaza de Armas, the square in front of the Cathedral.

FOREIGN DIPLOMATIC CORPS.

United States of America. Phillip Morgan, Minister Plenipotentiary and Envoy Extraordinary, No. 2 San Diego Street. Secretary of Legation, Harry H. Morgan.

Belgium. George Neyt, Minister Resident, No. 12 First San Francisco Street. Secretary of Legation, Adolfo du Chastel de la Houardies.

Chili. Domingo Gana, Minister Plenipotentiary and Envoy Extraordinary, Calle Cadena. Secretary of Legation, Guillermo Edwards.

France. Gustave de Coutouly, Minister Plenipotentiary and Envoy Extraordinary, No. 2 Buena Vista. Secretary of the Embassy, Hunges Bonlard. Chancellor of Legation, Mr. Villard.

Germany. Baron de Walcker Gotter, Minister Resident. Secretary of Legation, Baron Ernest Wedell.

Guatemala, San Salvador, and Honduras. Manuel Herrera, Minister Plenipotentiary and Envoy Extraordinary, No. 8 San Ildefonso Street.

Italy. Ernesto Martuscelli, Minister Resident, No. 2 Buena Vista.

Spain. Guillermo Crespo, Minister Plenipotentiary and Envoy Extraordinary, No. 2 San Diego. Secretary of Legation, Andres Freuiler.

FOREIGN CONSULS.

United States of America, David H. Strother, No. 5 Perpetua Street; Belgium, Diedrich Grane, 14 San Agustin; Colombia, Jose de Ansoategui, 3 Empedradillo; Denmark, German F. Wichers, 17 San Agustin; Germany, Pablo Kosidowski, 7 Capuchinas; Guatemala, Rafael Gonzalez Hoz; Spain, Jose Perignat, Hotel Iturbide; Switzerland, Albert Kienast, 2 Monterilla Street.

HOTELS AND RESTAURANTS.

Bazar, Calle del Espíritu Santo, a central family hotel; French spoken; rooms from $1.00 to $2.00 per day. French restaurant with private saloons and garden; 75 cents per meal, and special terms per week or month.

Bella Union, corner of Calle de la Palma. Restaurant and boarding-house on the American system, kept by Miss Hube, Calle del Espíritu Santo, número 4; English, French, and Spanish spoken.

Europa, Calle del Coliseo Viejo, a Mexican hotel.

Gillow Hotel and Restaurant, Calle de San José el Real; a family hotel in a central situation; English, French, and Spanish spoken.

Gran Sociedad, Calle del Espíritu Santo ; Mexican hotel and restaurant.

Gual, Calle del Paente del Espíritu Santo; Mexican hotel.

Nacional, Calle de la Profesa or 3 de San Francisco.
Refugio, Calle del Refugio; Mexican hotel and restaurant (*fonda*).
San Agustin, hotel and restaurant (*fonda*), Mexican, Calle de San Agustin.
San Cárlos, Mexican hotel and restaurant, Calle del Coliseo.
Coliseo Viejo, fonda y hotel del Turco.
German Fonda, Callejon de Santa Clara.

La Concordia, café and restaurant; A. Omarini, proprietor; pastry and ice-creams; corner of Second Calle de Plateros and San José el Real; French cooking; *déjeuners à la fourchette, diners à la carte*, and parties; saloon and private cabinets; English, French, Italian, and Spanish spoken.

Tivolis, de Bucareli, del Eliseo, del Ferrocarril, de San Cósme, kept by Porras; Petit Versailles, from $1.00 to $10.00 *déjeuner à la fourchette*, or *diner*, and wines.

Iturbide, Second Calle de San Francisco, for single ladies and gentlemen; English, French, and Spanish spoken; rooms from $3.00 per day; special terms for permanent boarders.

French Restaurant, in the Iturbide Hotel, and superintended by its owner, M. C. Recamier. A breakfast or dinner here costs in the main saloon, at private tables, from $1.00 upwards, and in the garden or private saloons, from $1.50.

THEATRES.

National, *Teatro Nacional* (first-class), Vergara Street; *Teatro Principal*, Coliseo Street; Arbeu Theatre; Alarcon, Arsénas Street; Merced Morales, Lerdo Avenue; Guerrero, Tenexpa Street; Autores, Baño del Jordan. Second-class: American, Hidalgo, Jordan, New Mexico, and Oriental.

BANKS.

Banco de Empleados, 5 San Agustin; Banco de Londres, Mexico and South America, 3 Capuchinas; Banco Mercantil, 15 San Agustin; Montepio.

PLAZAS AND PASEOS.

There are nearly five hundred miles of streets, which intersect at right angles; and throughout the city are numerous squares, *plazas* or *placitas*. The most important is the Plaza Mayor, the great square near the centre of the city, on one side of which is the great cathedral; on another, the National Palace; on another, the municipal buildings; and in the centre, the Zocalo, a beautiful garden, densely shaded, with a music-stand, statues, fountains, etc. From this point the street-railways take their departure, and the attractive flower-market is held here. It is a point at which, also, the historic interest is greater than at any other, as it covers the site of the ancient Aztec temples and armories.

The Plazuela of San Domingo is next in interest, having the fine old church of San Domingo, the buildings of the Inquisition, and the custom-house.

The various market-squares are exceedingly attractive, especially the great enclosed one near the Palace, where every article essential to Mexican economy is displayed for sale, including all the fruits of the country.

The principal street, upon or near which are the rich stores, is the Calle de San Francisco, leading from the Plaza Mayor to the beautiful Alameda, or botanical garden, which is a favorite resting-place for all, strangers and citizens alike. The grandest avenue of Mexico, the Pasco Grande, runs straight away towards Chapultepec, an avenue ornamented with trees and statuary, and dividing the great tract of land purchased by the Mexico Hotel and Land Company, in the centre of which they purpose erecting a most magnificent hotel for American tourists and residents. Even at this late day, with direct rail communication with the North, Mexico has no hotel adequate to the demands already made by visiting Americans. The Paseo de Bucarelli diverges from nearly the same point as the great avenue, and has some objects worthy of attention.

Of streets in general, that leading to Tacuba is bristling with historic objects; and the paseo of La Vega, running along the canal of the same name, is a favorite promenade, and a fine place in which to study the costumes and peculiarities of the Aztec boatman coming in to early market from the floating gardens.

CHURCHES, MUSEUMS, LIBRARIES, ETC.

Above the site of the ancient Aztec *teocalli* stands the great and world-famous cathedral, begun in 1573, and completed in 1657. Grand and imposing as is its exterior, its interior is magnificent, resplendent with gilding, rich in altar-rails, pictures, chapels, balustrades of fine metal, statues, and carvings. Entrance can be obtained at any time to the body of the cathedral, and to the great towers (200 feet high), and to the inner sanctuary, where the treasures are kept, by the payment of a small fee.

Of other religious edifices, the Church of San Domingo, San Hypolito, and a dozen more, will well repay examination. The leading Protestant church is the Methodist, on Calle Gante: the finest is the Church of Jesus, Calle San Francisco. The celebrated Calendar Stone is to be seen cemented into the western wall of the cathedral.

The great museum, in the Palace collection of buildings, should demand a large portion of the visitor's time, as it contains famous relics of the past, such as the Sacrificial Stone, statues of the Aztec god of war and numerous others, vast collections of pottery, portraits of famous Mexicans and viceroys, and a multitude of objects unique and interesting. Near this museum is the Academy of San Carlos, with its valuable collection of paintings and statuary. Entrance can be obtained to either upon application at the gates, and on certain days both are open to the public. The finest library in Mexico is the Biblioteca Nacional, in a magnificent structure, the renovated Convent of San Augustin: it contains over 100,000 volumes. The College of Mines, an immense building, is on the street of San Andres.

The mint, from which has issued forth so many millions of Mexican silver, can be inspected as desired; and the National Palace, containing the Senate Chambers, the Meteorological Observatory, and many relics of Mexico's past, is courteously opened to visitors, upon proper representation.

The Post-Office is in the Calle de Moneda; the Palace of Congress, in Calle del Factor; the Palace of Justice, in Cordobanes.

SUBURBAN VILLAGES, ETC.

The entire Mexican valley bristles with objects of antiquity, churches, or villages, connected with its fascinating history.

The nearest suburb is Guadalupe, reached by tramway (two miles), where is the famous sanctuary to the Virgin Guadalupe, begun in 1622, and built at a cost of $800,000; gifts to which, including sixty lamps of silver and a silver tabernacle, reached a fabulous amount. A chapel on the hill above was built about a hundred years later: it overlooks the spot where the Virgin is said to have appeared to an Indian, in 1531, and there is here a fine mineral spring. The famous blanket with the miraculous image of the Virgin stamped upon it, the battle-flag of Hidalgo, and the bones of some good viceroys, are deposited in the temple. An annual pilgrimage is made here Dec. 12, when all the Indians assemble to do homage to the only Indian saint in the calendar. The treaty of 1848, between the United States and Mexico, was signed here.

On the other side of the city is Chapultepec, with the finest groves of cypress in the country, surrounding a low hill upon which is perched the castle, stormed by the Americans in 1847, occupied by Maximilian, and now used as an astronomical observatory. One of the great aqueducts supplying Mexico starts from here; the other, from El Desierto, a delightful wood fifteen miles from the city. Molino del Rey is just back of Chapultepec; Churubusco is on the main diligence road to the south; Contreras and the Pedregal (other points famous in the Mexican war) are near San Angel, reached by tramway, as also is Tacubaya, a suburban town with gardens and fine views. The bull-ring, where fights go on every Sunday and feast-day, is just outside the limits of the Federal district, about one and one-half miles from Chapultepec. Tacuba, a small town on the northern causeway, is reached by tramway from the Plaza Mayor. At Popotla, a near village, is the sacred tree of *Noche Triste*, beneath which, it is said, Cortes sat him down, and wept at his great losses, when driven from the city in 1520. The American cemetery, the aqueduct, and the bridge of Alvarado, are all on this road, near which, before the city limits are passed, is the Cemetario of San Fernando, with its honored dead. The baths, hot and mineral, of El Peñon, are about two miles from the city, beyond the San Lazaro gate; while most extensive ones, with every convenience, are near the Grand Paseo.

The various bazaars, with their thousand and one *curios*, are a never-ending source of entertainment, also the stores of the silversmiths, dealers in wax figures, *sombreros* and *sarapes:* they are everywhere, and need not be designated.

Historic Tezcoco, seat of ancient empire, place whence Cortes invested Mexico, containing some ruins of interest, is reached by rail by the *Ferrocarril Interoceanico*, in an hour and a half; Chalco, almost equally celebrated, in two hours; by the same road, Amecameca, in three hours and a half, — an attractive town, with a celebrated Sacro Monte (or sacred mount). Here the trail is taken for the summit of Popocatepetl, highest volcano in Mexico, fifteen miles distant. Taking the morning train, making arrangements in Ameca with the merchants Noriega Mijares, for horses, donkeys, guides, and provisions, one can ascend to the rancho at the snow-limit, before night, thence to the peak, and return next day, if desired. For a mountain of its height, Popocatepetl is comparatively easy of ascent; yet it will be best to provide one's self with a stout staff, heavy shoes, colored glasses, and abundant provisions. For further details, the reader is referred to "Travels in Mexico," Chap. XX. There are three hotels in Ameca, — Ferrocarril, Barcelona, and Neria.

The most conspicuous ancient monuments near Mexico city are the Pyramids of San Juan Teotihuacan, about forty miles; leave the Mexican Railway at station of San Juan, and hire a guide in the village, a short distance from station.

At Cuernavaca, reached by diligence, — a day's ride, — one may find most picturesque scenery, a semi-tropical climate, and vast sugar-estates. Good hotels are here. Beyond, over a rough road, horseback, are the ruins of Xochicalco, half a day, and the famous cavern of Cacahuamilpa, two days. The diligence-office is in the rear of Hotel Iturbide, Mexico City.

An excursion by rail to Toluca, over the Mexican National Road, now finished as far as the quaint little city of Morelia, 378 kilometres, and fifteen hours, would include these celebrated places, and also Indian towns of importance, such as Maravatio and Acámbaro, as well as views of forests, and mines of gold and silver.

We have thus outlined merely, the principal points of interest in and near Mexico city, showing that its list of attractions is not a short one.[1] Good guide-books are numerous, giving them all in detail; while guides and couriers are always ready at the principal hotels; and the number of Americans resident in the city, speaking the language of the country, and ever courteous in their attentions to a stranger, makes it an easy matter for him to "do" the valley without loss of time or temper.

---

[1] With the opening of the first Mexican season, the well-known excursion managers, Messrs. Raymond and Whitcomb (who have successfully conducted so many large parties to California and the various resorts of the United States), will turn their attention towards Mexico. It will be especially grateful to tourists to be accompanied by guides and interpreters through a country which is essentially foreign, and to have every want provided for in advance, from beginning to end of journey; and the writer takes pleasure in calling attention to the forthcoming Raymond Excursions to Mexico.

ROUTE II.

BOSTON, NEW YORK, OR CHICAGO, TO ST. LOUIS, as in Route I., thence to City of Mexico, via the Missouri Pacific System and connections.

(A)   TEXAS PACIFIC AND MEXICAN CENTRAL.

From	To.	Distance.	Time.
St. Louis	El Paso (Texas Pacific)	1,358 miles.	66 hours.
El Paso	City of Mexico (Mexican Central)	1,225 miles.	60 hours.
From El Paso, south, as in	Route 1 (A).		
		2,583 miles.	126 hours.

(B)   MISSOURI PACIFIC SYSTEM AND MEXICAN NATIONAL.

From.	To.	Distance.	Time.
St. Louis	Laredo (Missouri Pacific)	1,150 miles.	57 hours.
Laredo	Saltillo (Mexican National)	234 miles.	13 hours.
Saltillo	San Miguel (by Diligence, 1884)	362 miles	5 days.
San Miguel	City of Mexico (Mexican National),	254 miles.	12 hours.
		2,000 miles.	

A TRIP THROUGH TEXAS.

While being rapidly whirled over the Texas prairies in the most luxurious of palace or dining cars, we shall be likely to forget, unless frequently reminded of it, that we are crossing the largest State in the Union.

Although our object is sight-seeing merely, yet as material resources influence progress, and that, in turn, provides comforts for the traveller, we should not omit to mention, that, while territorially vast, Texas also contains a great variety of soil, and consequent vegetation; its crops of cotton, cane, and cereals, being enormous, while its prairies annually sustain over 4,000,000 cattle. Its area of 274,350 square miles is greater by over 30,000 square miles than the Empire of Aus-

RIVER VIEW, SAN ANTONIO.
(*Missouri-Pacific Ry*)

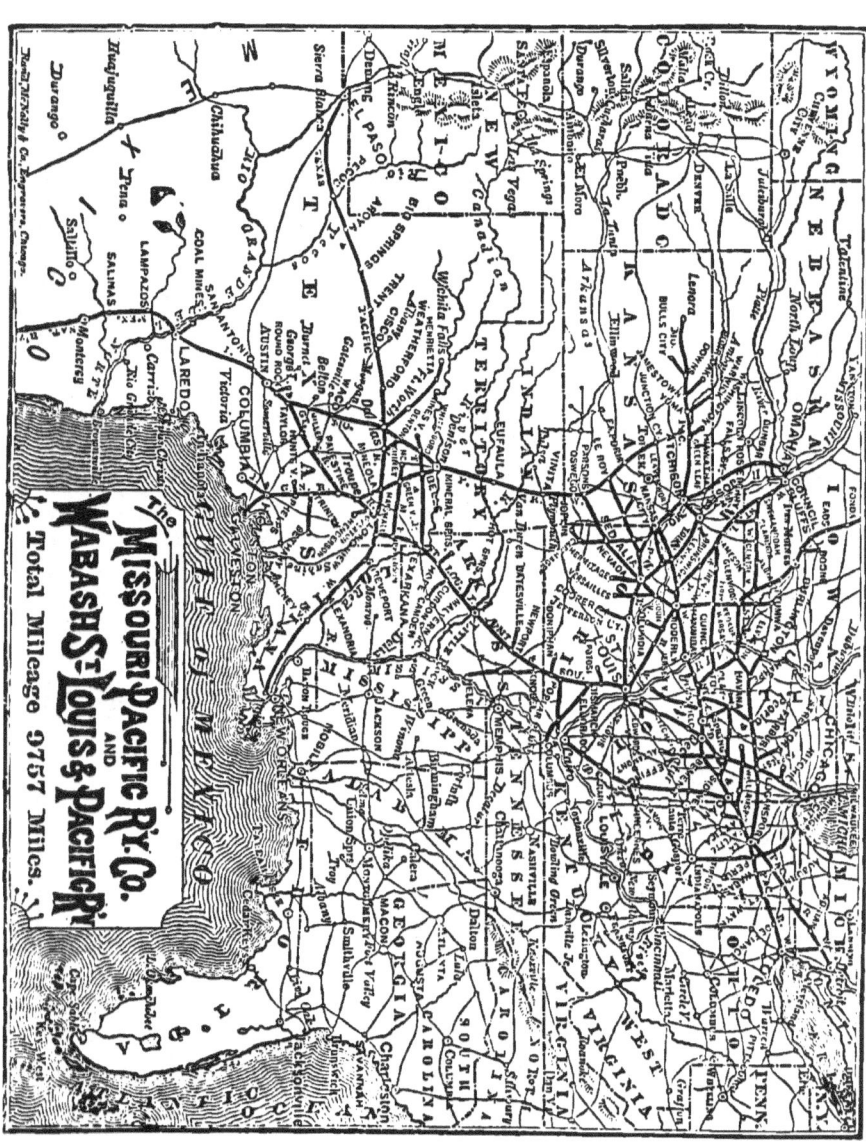

ANTIQUITIES OF SAN ANTONIO, TEX.

tria, exceeds the German Empire by 62,000 square miles; while Great Britain and Ireland would form merely an oasis in one of its deserts. A native-born Texan could (and cheerfully would) add to these figures a mass of statistics showing that his State had the largest school-fund in the world, more miles of wire fence, more millions of acres awaiting a population, more fertile soil, and a finer climate, than any other country of the globe. While rather dubious about its soil, taking the territory as a whole, we can conscientiously commend its climate. From Austin its capital, southward, it improves in rarity and diathermancy, until at San Antonio we find a delightful temperature, faulty only from local causes.

At Austin we enter a rolling region, famous for its woods, vales, and delightful vegetation, on the border of a land where the winter climate is tempered to the requirements of invalids who cannot endure the harsher temperature of the North. As the capital of the State, it is a centre of social refinement; and its architecture is ambitious. Good hotels here render a stay of any length agreeable. But at San Antonio, forty-eight hours from St. Louis, the tourist in search of winter sunbeams is likely to linger longest; for, at the height of six hundred feet above the Gulf of Mexico, the humid coast atmosphere is deprived of its superfluous burden of moisture, and is soft, yet exhilarating.

Through the quaint old city flows a beautiful river, crossed in many places by bridges, bubbling up here and there in wonderful springs, now laving the banks of a smooth and ever-verdant lawn, then plunging into the sombre depths of a live-oak wood. Aside from the tree-fringed river that pursues its sinuous course through the very heart of the city, there are other streams equally attractive; and springs burst out everywhere through the limestone, especially in its park, San Pedro, where they are most numerous, and create a very paradise of flower and foliage by their tepid waters. Overlooking the city, on a hill, are the fine buildings of the United States military department; this place having long been occupied as headquarters, owing to its salubrity, and central and commanding location. Many of the most attractive resorts of San Antonio can be reached by horse-cars from the central plaza, about which are the best hotels. Here, likewise, is that building so famous in the sanguinary struggle for Texan independence,—the ALAMO. This old structure, whose walls were baptized in the blood of heroes, has been purchased by the State, and can be freely examined by all visitors. Nearly opposite is the Mexican Cathedral, worth a visit. But by far the most interesting relics of Mexican architecture are the celebrated mission-buildings, scattered along the river-bank, from a mile to several miles distant. San José and San Juan are most famous structures, not alone being ancient, but possessing architectural beauties in carven pillars, windows, and cornices that no modern buildings can rival. The halo of antiquity and of a most fascinating history lingers about them, and by no means should one of them be omitted from the tourist's itinerary.

So it is that San Antonio gives us a hint of Mexico, in its bland climate, in the costumes of its Mexican population, in the architecture of its ancient buildings.

Connection is made here, as well as at Austin, with New Orleans and Houston, and with Galveston,—that thriving city on the sands, with its grand hotel, fine drives, and delightful sea-bathing.

Nine hours south of San Antonio, after a good night's rest in a luxurious "sleeper," we reach Laredo, and make change for cars of the Mexican National, a narrow-gauge road which runs as far (1884) as Saltillo,—234 miles. A day could be well spent in Laredo, although it is not especially attractive; for here the Rio Grande is first seen, and on the opposite bank is the thoroughly Mexican town of Nuevo Laredo, a typical mud village with many interesting peculiarities. The Gulf of Mexico may be reached (160 miles distant) over the northern division of the Mexican National to Corpus Christi, where is excellent sea-bathing, and vast ranches, with abundant game — antelope, deer, etc. — in sections on the way.

CONVENT OF SAN FRANCISCO, MONTEREY.
(*Loaned by Missouri-Pacific Ry.*)

The ride to Monterey is unrelieved by notable scenery, and does not reveal a single town of importance. Halfway on, the blue and beautiful mountains appear in sight; and a singular *mesa*, or table-topped hill, claims attention, with here and there scattered groups of upland palms and maguey-plants. At Villadama a Mexican meal is served; and the monotony of the trip thence is unbroken until Monterey is reached, at four P.M.

MONTEREY.

Hacks are in waiting for every train (fare, twenty-five cents to the city, a mile distant), and good horse-cars (fare, ten cents).

There are two hotels here, the Iturbide and Monterey, both in Mexican style, single-storied, built around an inner quadrilateral court. After the arid stretches below, Monterey is a glad surprise: surrounded by mountains, and at an elevation of 1,600 feet, its climate is extremely agreeable. Near it are several thermal and mineral springs, which contribute to its claims as a health-resort. The buildings are all in Mexican style. Its public structures are fine. It has many *plazas*, the largest and most beautiful being the Plaza of Zaragoza, the fountain in which is of marble, sculptured in dolphins' and lions' heads.

Objects of interest: the Plaza; Cathedral; the Church and Convent of the Franciscans; a large unfinished temple, — *La Basilica Laterneuse*; the *Casa Municipal*, or City Hall; the State Palace; the Library; the Parian, or great bazaar; and in the suburbs, the ruins of the Black Fort, captured by the Americans in 1847; *El Obispado*, or Bishop's Palace, on a hill commanding a magnificent view; the Cemetery; *El Capillo*, or chapel, across the river; the two picturesque mountains,

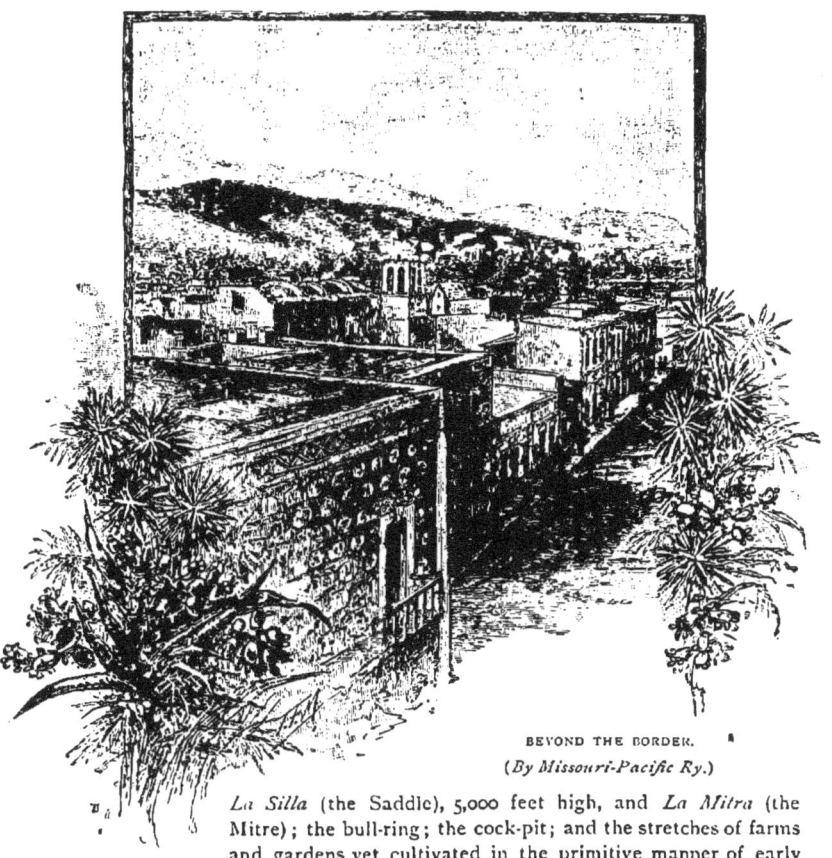

BEYOND THE BORDER.
(*By Missouri-Pacific Ry.*)

La Silla (the Saddle), 5,000 feet high, and *La Mitra* (the Mitre); the bull-ring; the cock-pit; and the stretches of farms and gardens yet cultivated in the primitive manner of early times. To a stranger, this city, founded three hundred years ago, and its inhabitants, will be exceedingly interesting, as both represent and are typical of the Mexico of six hundred miles beyond.

SALTILLO.

A place yet more charming is Saltillo, sixty-seven miles farther, on the slopes of the table-land, among the mountains, yet with soft airs, blooming gardens, orchards, fields, springs, and streams. Its great Plaza, with its flowers and trees, as well as the entire city, is supplied with pure spring-water, conducted from the hilltops. The great Cathedral, covering an entire block, and with sculptured front, faces the Plaza; other churches, of all denominations, are here; and the theatre, bull-ring, and *alameda* furnish recreation and enjoyment. A fine hotel, the San Estevan, is in charge of Americans. The city government is in honest and friendly hands, and every thing promises well for the opening of Saltillo as an attractive resort, either for summer or winter.

Below Saltillo is *La Encantada*, the Enchanted Valley; and seven miles out is Buena Vista, near which place Gen. Taylor defeated Santa Anna. The country beyond has no cities of any size, except Venado, a small manufacturing place, and consists of vast plains bounded by mountains, the road running through *haciendas* of immense extent, with an infrequent village, and halting-places where meals are served to the travellers by the diligence.

SAN LUIS POTOSI,

a city isolate in the great plains, soon to be connected by rail with the United States and with the gulf-port of Tampico, contains many fine public buildings, notable being the Palace of Justice and Governor's Palace, the Cathedral, churches of el Carmen, San Augustine, San Francisco, and la Merced, colleges of advanced grades, the usual *plazas*, and narrow, picturesque streets, with hotels as yet only in the Mexican style.

Southward, in the track of the railroad, lie vast *haciendas*, such as Jaral, which once controlled 20,000 peons, and whose owner furnished a full regiment of cavalry to aid the royalists against the Mexican insurgents.

Dolores Hidalgo, a small place, is celebrated in Mexican revolutionary history; for here the patriot Hidalgo first sounded the watchword of liberty that eventually spread over all Mexico. San Miguel is a larger city, with about 20,000 inhabitants, with neat churches and fine squares; while curious Indian villages are scattered all along the route. At Celaya, a city of about 30,000 inhabitants, the National crosses the Central; and the journey can be pursued either by way of Acámbaro and Toluca, 200 miles, or by the Mexican Central (Route I.), 180 miles, *via* Queretaro and Tula, to the city of Mexico.

ROUTE III.
TO CITY OF MEXICO, FROM THE EAST, VIA NEW ORLEANS.

Distance, 2,250 miles; time, 7 days.

Several all-rail routes are open to New Orleans, either *via* Pennsylvania Railroad through Washington, and Southern connections by way of Danville and Atlanta, or south from Cincinnati. Connections at New Orleans for Texas and Mexico.

By the most direct route, the Piedmont Air Line, it is 1,374 miles from New York to New Orleans, and 54 hours through-time.

A varied and delightful trip, embracing a sea-voyage also, may be made by steam from Boston (Boston and Savannah Steamship Company), sailing every Thursday, and connecting with trains (two daily) the following Monday for New Orleans (26 hours, and 576 miles). Connections are made here with the all-rail line to the Pacific and Mexico, and with steamers to Galveston and Vera Cruz. By this line of travel, Florida may be visited *en route*.

THE NEW ORLEANS AND MEXICAN STEAMSHIP LINE.

Distance, 876 miles: time (direct), 4 1-2 days.

From New Orleans to Vera Cruz there are two lines, the Morgan and the Alexandre, making the round trip every twenty-one days. The steamer touches, going and coming, at the Mexican ports of Bagdad, Tampico, and Tuxpan, and arrives at Vera Cruz on the morning of the sixth day after leaving New Orleans.

Bagdad, situated at the mouth of the Rio Grande, is the seaport of the city of Matamoras, and is the first stopping-place on the outward trip; and the run from Bagdad to the mouth of the Panuco River, upon whose left bank the city and seaport of Tampico is situated, is about thirty hours.

As there are seldom more than eight feet of water on the bar of the river, and the water shoals considerably near the coast, the steamer is compelled to anchor about two miles off shore, and discharge her cargo into lighters. During the winter months, frequent "northers" blow with great violence along the entire Mexican gulf-coast; and, as there is not a single well-protected harbor along the entire gulf, sailing-vessels, and very often steamers also, are compelled to up anchor, and run to sea.

The Central Railroad Company is engaged in constructing a railroad from Tampico to San Luis Potosi, the capital of the rich mining State of the same name; and, when this is completed, all the varied products of the tropical and semi-tropical countries through which it passes will be brought to Tampico for shipment to foreign markets. From Tampico to Tuxpan is 125 miles. Here, also, the seaport is situated on the bank of a river some distance from the coast; and, as at Tampico the bar of the river carries but little water, the ship lies off the mouth of the river about two miles from the bar. The products of the country in the vicinity of Tuxpan are sugar, molasses, honey, rice, vanilla, cedar and other woods, rubber, and many kinds of tropic fruits.

The colonists (including an American colony of about six hundred persons) are engaged principally in planting and in cutting cedar and dye-woods. Most of these products go to Northern ports, particularly the dye-woods and cedar; which latter, however, finds its best market in Europe.

From Tuxpan to Vera Cruz the distance by sea is 120 miles. The steamers leave the Tuxpan roadstead late in the evening, and arrive at the port of Vera Cruz about seven the next morning. Here, also, the ship receives and discharges her cargo by means of lighters, although she lies but about a half-mile from the mole, within a few yards of the celebrated fortress of San Juan de Ulua. At this city, the terminus of the line, the steamer connects with the New-York line, owned by the same company, and which touches at the ports of Frontera, Campeche, Progreso, and Havana.

The Morgan Line makes the round trip between Morgan City and Vera Cruz twice a month, leaving Morgan City on the 1st, arriving at Vera Cruz on the 5th; returning, leaves Vera Cruz on the 8th, and reaches Morgan City on the evening of the 12th, which port it leaves again for Vera Cruz on the 16th, etc., touching at Galveston both ways.

A GATEWAY, VERA CRUZ.

Palmer-Sullivan Concession.
MEXICAN NATIONAL RAILWAY.

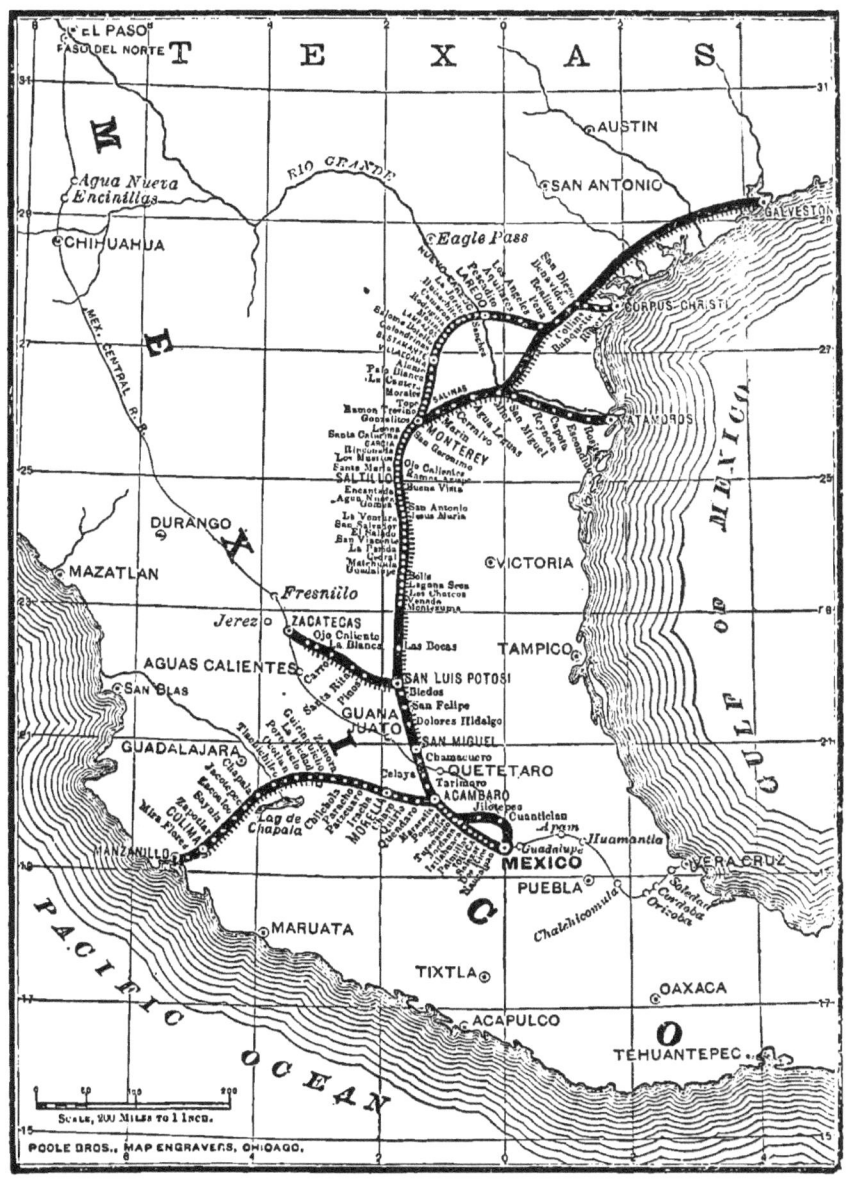

DOUBLE·DAILY·TRAINS
VIRGINIA
OR
Richmond
&
Danville
ROUTE
THE NORTH

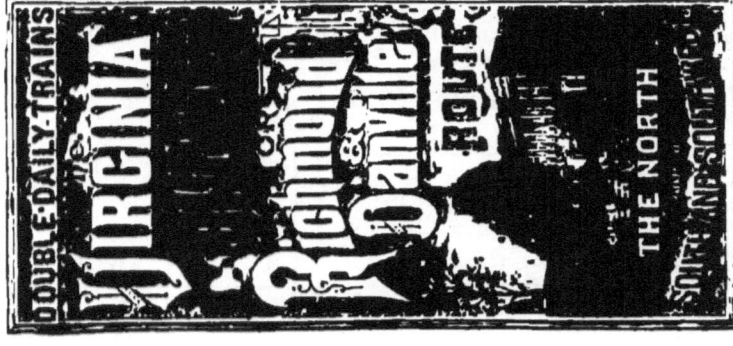

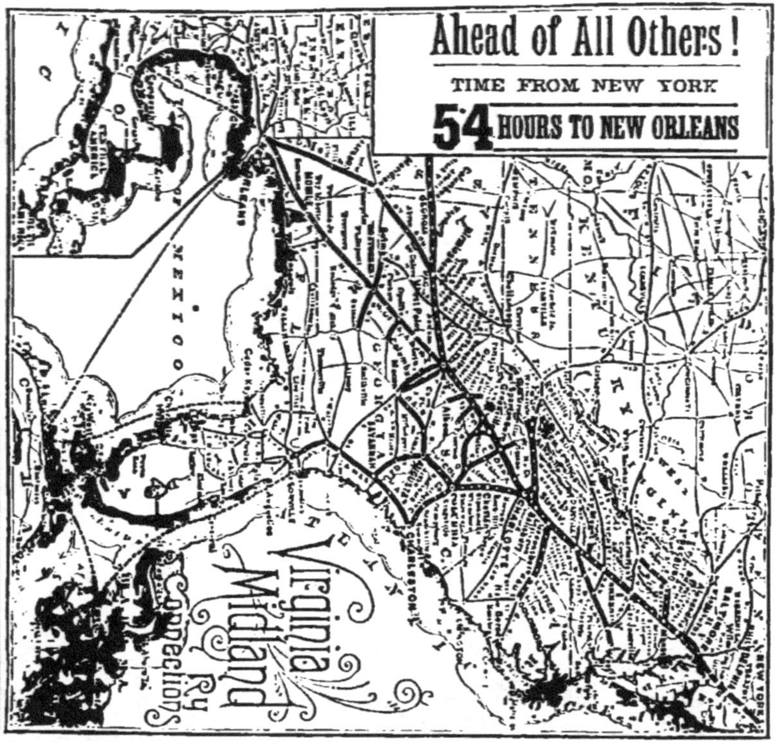
Ahead of All Others!
TIME FROM NEW YORK
54 HOURS TO NEW ORLEANS
Virginia
Midland
Ry
Connections
MEXICO
CHARLESTON
NEW YORK

ROUTE IV.
BY SEA via CUBA AND YUCATAN, MEXICAN RAILWAY TO CITY OF MEXICO.

	Distance.	Time.
New York to Havana	1,187 miles.	4 days.
	At Havana,	1 day.
Havana to Progreso (Yucatan)	426 miles.	1½ days.
	At Progreso,	1 day.
Progreso to Vera Cruz	388 miles.	1½ days.
	2,001 miles.	9 days.
Vera Cruz to City of Mexico	. . . .	14 hours.

In speaking of Mexico, we naturally presuppose that the capital is meant; and it is with the CITY OF MEXICO as an objective point that these descriptions of routes are written. Ten days' voyaging, and two thousand miles, intervene between New York and Vera Cruz, principal seaport of Mexico.

THE ALEXANDRE STEAMERS.

A fleet of large iron steamers connects New York with the only port of any size on the Mexican coast. These steamers call at Havana, four days out, and reach the first Mexican port, at Progreso, on the peninsula of Yucatan, two days later. Two of these boats, the "City of Alexandria" and "City of Washington," are the finest of any engaged in coastwise commerce. They are over 300 feet in length, 38 feet wide, and 33 feet deep, are built of iron, and furnished throughout with every convenience and comfort that can be found upon the great ocean-steamers between this country and Europe. Each has superb accommodations for 150 first-class passengers, and, in place of the common tables usually found in our coast steamers, has small tables, at which four persons can dine or lunch *a la carte*, at any hour. The saloons are immense, and finished beautifully in fine woods, showing every color, from black walnut to amaranth. A seventh steamer was launched in 1882, the "City of Puebla," that was intended to surpass, if possible, all the others of the fleet.

After leaving Progreso, these steamers touch successively at Campeche and Frontera, arriving at Vera Cruz in from ten to twelve days, whence, after remaining four days, they return to New York. Coming down from New Orleans are two steamers of the same line, which touch at Bagdad, Tampico, and Tuxpan, reaching Vera Cruz inside of five days. The journey there might be shortened, if long delays were not made in every port. Eight days by the sea-route, and six *via* New Orleans, ought to cover it; but generally the passenger welcomes these stays in port as opportunities for side trips into the country. The rates of passage are as follows: From New York to Vera Cruz, first-class, $85; excursion, good for six months, $150; New Orleans to Vera Cruz, $50; excursion, $80.

It is at Progreso, on the coast of Yucatan, that the steamer first enters

Mexican dominion, and the low-lying coast presents itself to view. This port is connected with the interior by a railroad to Merida, the capital of the State of Yucatan, whence other roads lead into a region growing more attractive year by year.

The fare from Progreso to Merida is one dollar; distance, twenty-six miles. The entire peninsula — its picturesque features, at least — has been so minutely described in the author's "Travels in Mexico," Chaps. I.-X., that nothing remains but to refer the reader to that work. Merida will be found quaint and attractive, and numerous excursions can be taken from this point to visit the wonderful ruins and hunting localities. Address Dr. George F. Gaumer, Merida, Yucatan, — a gentleman who has hunted throughout the length of the peninsula, — for particulars.

THE MOAT, VERA CRUZ.

Aside from points reached by the interior railways, the following ancient and interesting places can be visited by *volan coché*, or private conveyance: Uxmal, 65 miles; fare, $20; Aké, 30 miles; fare, $15; Mayapan, 30 miles; fare, $15; Izamal, 45 miles (mail-wagon); fare, $7; Chichen Itza, 120 miles; fare, $50.

Hotels are scarce, but the people of Yucatan are hospitable.

Passing on the way Campeche and Frontera, ports of call, off which the steamers generally lie long enough to give opportunity for visiting the shore, they anchor at Vera Cruz, under the walls of the great island-fortress, San Juan de Ulua. Boats convey passengers to land (fare, fifty cents), where luggage is examined with little delay. Good hotels are numerous, at about three dollars per day; also restaurants. Objects of interest: Custom-House, main Plaza, old Convent, and the great Fort. A ride in the street-cars into the suburbs will display nearly all of the attractions of Vera Cruz, and a day or so exhaust them all.

Other steam-lines centring here from foreign countries are : the German Line to Havre and Hamburg, monthly; the Royal Mail, monthly, to Plymouth and Southampton; Spanish Line, monthly, to Spain; French Line, monthly, to St. Nazaire, etc.; a Mexican Line to home ports on the Gulf.

From Vera Cruz to the city of Mexico, distant 263 miles, and 14 hours, runs the great line known as the Mexican Railway.[1]

A branch line also runs to Jalapa, seventy miles, a most delightful town in the mountains, passing over the ancient royal road, and through the pass of Cerro Gordo. This trip should not be omitted.

The entire journey, from the coast to the valley of Mexico, is through grand and picturesque scenery, giving every variety of vegetation as the mountains are ascended, crossing numerous bridges, spanning ravines and barrancas, and with snow-covered Orizaba ever in sight, even over the fields of sugarcane and coffee, and banana-gardens.

Cordova, sixty-five miles from Vera Cruz, presents a charming blending of tropical and temperate scenery and climate, and is in the centre of the coffee region. Its hotels are poor.

Orizaba, eighty-two miles, has better hotels and many attractions, including fine streams, mountain-views, and an interesting architecture and people.

Maltrata is in a beautiful mountain valley, above which the track climbs to the crest of the table-land at Boca del Monte.

At Esperanza, 111 miles, a narrow-gauge railway connects for Tehuacan, a town worth visiting, whence a diligence runs a day's journey southward, towards Oaxaca, the birthplace of Diaz and Juarez, a city of 27,000, extremely interesting, and with fascinating ruins lying about it. To reach it requires three days' travel on horseback, besides one day in the diligence. Horses must be ordered in advance. No hotels on the route, but fair ones in Oaxaca.

At Apizaco, 176 miles, a branch leads off to the beautiful city of Puebla, with 70,000, with a host of attractions,—a grand cathedral with magnificent interior, libraries, baths, bull-ring, fair hotels, and fine buildings. Six miles distant by tramway is the famous Pyramid of Cholula, with its ancient town, containing many buildings of early date. All about is spread a mountainous country, enveloping fertile plains. Three great mountains, including Popocatepetl, are near to Puebla and Cholula.

At Irolo, 215 miles, another line runs northward to Pachuca, a mining centre worked from the years of the Conquest, where are the famous Real del Monte mines, and others of note. There are good hotels here. It is a delightful day's journey from Vera Cruz to Mexico City,—one so filled with varied scenes, that its like may not be found elsewhere in America. Trains enter the suburb of Buena Vista, whence conveyances (as described on p. 18) take passengers to the city.

---

[1] Vera Cruz and the ascent to Mexico fully described in Travels in Mexico, Chap. XXII.

ROUTE V.

SAN FRANCISCO, CAL., TO CITY OF MEXICO, via SOUTHERN PACIFIC RAILROAD TO EL PASO, AND MEXICAN CENTRAL.

Time, San Francisco to El Paso, 58 hours: El Paso to Mexico City, 60 hours = 118 hours.
Distance, San Francisco to El Paso, 1,286 miles: El Paso to Mexico City, 1,225 miles = 2,511 miles.
At Benson, on Southern Pacific Railroad, connection is made with Guaymas, Gulf of California.
Local fares by this route are ten cents per mile.

ROUTE VI.

SAN FRANCISCO TO MEXICO (WEST COAST), via PACIFIC MAIL STEAMERS.

Distance, San Francisco to Port of Mazatlan . . . . 1,165 miles.
Distance, San Francisco to Manzanillo . . . . 1,456 miles.
Distance, San Francisco to Acapulco . . . . 1,607 miles.
Distance, San Francisco to Salina Cruz (Tehuantepec) . . . . 1,895 miles.
Distance, San Francisco to San José (Guatemala) . . . . 2,196 miles.
Distance, San Francisco to Panama (Isthmus) . . . . 3,198 miles.
Distance, San Francisco to New York (touching at Mexican ports) . . . . 5,220 miles.

Time between San Francisco and New York, about twenty-nine days, — twenty days on the Pacific, and nine on the Atlantic.

Fares, the same as by rail across the continent.

Acapulco is the finest port of Mexico on the Pacific, in the State of Guerrero, about 190 miles south-west of Mexico City, in latitude north, 16° 55'; longitude, 99° 48' west. Population, 3,000.

"It was not discovered," says R. A. Wilson, "when Cortés built, in Colima, the vessels that went to search for a north-west passage; but, when they had returned from their fruitless search, they anchored in the mountain-girt harbor of Acapulco. The discoveries of the celebrated navigator Magellan fixed the commercial character and importance of this seaport. He had sailed through the straits that bear his name, and coasted northwardly as far as the Trades, and from thence he bore away to the Spice Islands, discovering on the voyage the Philippine Islands, where the city of Manila was founded. By this voyage he demonstrated that the advantages of a route across the Pacific were so superior to a voyage around Cape Horn, as to justify the expense of a land transit from Acapulco to Vera Cruz, and reshipment to Spain.

"The practical advantage of this discovery was the establishment of the annual Manila galleon, in which was sent out $1,000,000 to purchase Oriental products for the consumption of Spain and all her American Colonies. In this galleon sailed the friars that went forth to the spiritual conquest of India. In it sailed Spanish soldiers, who followed hard after the priests, to add the temporal to the spiritual subjugation of Oriental empires. To this harbor the galleon returned, freighted with the rich merchandise of China, Japan, and the Spice Islands. When the arrival of the galleon was announced, traders hastened from every quarter of New Spain to attend the annual fair. Little vessels from down the coast came to get their share of the mammoth cargo. The king's officers came to look after the royal revenue; and caravans of mules were summoned to transport the Spanish portion of the freight to Vera Cruz.

"Such was the commercial condition of the town down to the time of the independence. From this time it was lost to commerce, until it was made a halfway house on the voyage to California. The town lies upon a narrow intervale between the hills and the harbor. It is built of the frailest materials, and is destroyed about once in ten years by an earthquake.

"The castle of San Diego stands upon a high bank; and the harbor appears like a nest scooped out of the mountains, into and out of which the tide ebbs and flows through a double channel riven by an earthquake in the solid rock. There is still another opening in the sharp mountain-ridge that encloses it from the sea; but this opening, dug by the labor of man, at a point opposite the entrance of the harbor, was to let the cool sea-breeze in upon one of the hottest and most unhealthy places upon the continent. Such, in substance, is and was the little city of Acapulco, the seat and focus of the Oriental commerce of New Spain."

This admirable description will apply to Acapulco of to-day, except that it would be well to add that the city awaits only the coming of the railroad from the city of Mexico, to awaken a revival of its lost commerce. The uniting of this port by rail with the gulf-port of Vera Cruz was the first object of railway projectors in Mexico; and this will at last be accomplished by the completion of the Morelos Railroad, through Amecameca, Cuernavaca, and Chilpancingo.

By road, the journey between this port and the capital consumes twelve days, over one of the worst trails in the country, worn by the feet of mules for the past three centuries.

ANCIENT AQUEDUCT, VERA CRUZ.

LIST OF ADVERTISEMENTS.

Raymond's Vacation Excursions	front cover, inside
Pope Bicycle Company	facing front cover, inside
National Tube Works (English)	fly leaf, page i
National Tube Works (Spanish)	fly leaf, page ii
Meisterschaft System	page facing title
Estes & Lauriat, Publishers	page facing title
Travelers' Insurance Company	page iv, facing "Mexican Resources"
Brown, Wood, & Kingman	page v (colored)
Nashua Hand Drill	page v "
Parker & Wood (Agricultural Implements)	page vi "
Parker & Wood (Agricultural Implements)	page vii "
Geo. Woods Company Parlor Organs	page viii "
Hamilton Manufacturing Company (Cottons)	page ix "
Fall River Line Steamers	page x "
Fuller & Holtzer (Electrical Supplies)	page x "
Blair Tourograph Company	page xi "
Boston & Savannah Steamship Company	page xi "
Geo. C. Richardson, Smith, & Company (Selling Agents)	page xii "
E. W. Vaill (Folding Chairs)	page xii "
G. H. Bushnell & Company (Knuckle-Joint Presses)	page xiii "
Webster's Dictionary ; Abogado Cristiano	page xiv "
Bell's Insect Exterminator: DeWitt C. Newell	page xiv "
Witherby, Rugg, & Richardson (Planing Machinery)	page xv "
G. H. Bushnell & Company (Spanish)	page xvi "
Washburn, Moen, & Company (Iron and Steel Wire)	page xvii "
Howard, Bullough, & Riley (Cotton Machinery)	page xviii "
Howard, Bullough, & Riley (Spanish)	page xix "
Fairbanks's Standard Scales	page xx "
Alexandre Steamship Company	facing page 19 of Guide
Lewis Engraving Company	facing back cover
Fitchburg Railroad	facing back cover
Leve & Alden (Tours and Excursions)	back cover, inside
Atchison, Topeka, and Santa Fe Railroad	back cover, outside

INDEX OF MAPS AND ILLUSTRATIONS.

	PAGE
Fitchburg Railroad	58
Horse Shoe Curve	59
Pennsylvania Railroad	60
Dining Car	Guide, 2
Chicago, Burlington, and Quincy Railroad	facing page 2
Drawing-room Car	3
Sleeping Car	4
On Santa Fé Trail	5
Las Vegas Hot Springs	6
Mexican Hut	7
The Rio Grande	10
Fountain at Chihuahua	12
Interior of *Adobe* Hut	14
Plan of City of Mexico	facing page 18
Market View	23
River View, San Antonio, Tex	24
Mexican Missions, San Antonio	facing page 24
Map of Missouri Pacific Railway	facing page 25
A Convent	26
Monterey, Mexico	27
Gateway, Vera Cruz	30
Map of Mexican National Railway	facing page 30
Map of Piedmont Air Line	facing page 31
The Moat, Vera Cruz	32
Ancient Aqueduct	35
Atchison, Topeka, and Santa Fé Railroad	back cover, outside

CONTENTS.

MEXICAN RESOURCES.

	PAGE
Area and Boundaries	1
Physical Features of Coast and Plateaux	2
Climate and Seasons; Mountains, Rivers, Lakes, etc.	3
Zones of Vegetation	4
Flora of Mexico	5
Timber and Construction Woods	6
Cabinet and Dye Woods	7
Cereals, Textile Plants, etc	8
Wild and Cultivated Fruits	9
Medicinal Plants	10
Flowers and Ornamental Plants	11
Aztec Agriculture	12, 13
Real Estate in Mexico; Seed-time and Harvest	14
Agriculture on the Table-land	15
Agriculture in the Hot Coast Region	16
Horse and Cattle Raising	17, 18
Sheep, Goats, and Swine	19
Irrigation and Improved Agriculture	20
Tables showing Annual Agricultural Productions	21
Special Products: Arrowroot, Banana, and Plantain	22
Cacao, Cactaceæ, Cassava, Chirimoya	23
Coca and Coco-palm	24
Coffee: Culture, Range, and Production	25, 26
Cotton: Ancient and Modern Cultivation; Amount produced	27
Henequen, or Sisal Hemp	28
Indigo, Cochineal, Maize, and Wheat	29
Rice, Sarsaparilla, and Vanilla	30
Sugar-cane: Cultivation and Production	31
Tobacco	32
Mineral Regions of Mexico	33
History of Mexican Mines	34
Ancient Mines of the Aztecs	35
The Great and Famous Mines	36
Total Product of Mexican Mines	37, 38, 39
Gold, when and where found	40
Silver, Principal Veins	41
Quicksilver	42
Iron, Copper, Lead, Sulphur, etc.	43
Precious Stones, Opals, etc.	44
Obsidian, Salt, Coals, and Mineral Oils	45
Mexican Process of reducing Ore	46–54
Annual Amount produced; Mining Nomenclature	55
Coinage of the Mexican Mints	56
Mexican Coins: Weights and Measures	57

A GUIDE TO MEXICO.

	PAGE
Distance and Time-tables from all Great Cities of the United States	1
To Mexico, via St. Louis	2
Westward, across the Great Plains	3
Across Kansas	4
In New Mexico	5
At Las Vegas Hot Springs	6, 7
Santa Fé; Railroads of New Mexico	8
Indians; the Pueblos	9
El Paso and the Rio Grande	10
Chihuahua, Durango, and Zacatecas	11
Mines of Zacatecas	12
Lagos, Leon, and Guanajuato	13, 14
The Baxio, Salamanca, Celaya	15
Queretaro	16
The Valley of Mexico	17
City of Mexico; Hacks and Street-railroads	18
Foreign Consuls; Hotels and Restaurants	19
Theatres, Banks, *Plazas* and *Paseos*	20
Churches, Museums, Libraries; Suburban Villages	21
Chapultepec, Guadalupe, Tezcoco, etc.	22
Historic Towns of the Valley	23
Distance and Time-tables across Texas	24
Austin and San Antonio	25
Monterey, Northern Mexico	26
Saltillo; Buena Vista Battle-ground	27
San Luis Potosi; down the Mexican Plateau	28
To Mexico City via New Orleans	29
Vera Cruz and the Gulf Coast	30
To Mexico via Cuba and Yucatan; the Alexandre Steamers	31
Yucatan and Vera Cruz	32
Cordova, Orizaba, Puebla, Pachuca	33
San Francisco to Mexico	34
Acapulco and West Coast of Mexico	35

www.ingramcontent.com/pod-product-compliance
Lightning Source LLC
Chambersburg PA
CBHW020144170426
43199CB00010B/886